THE DIY

GUIDE TO

N   G

for Small Chari—es
and Volunta
Organisatio s

Moi Ali

A DIRECTORY OF SOCIAL CHANGE PUBLICATION

A Directory of Social Change Publication

THE DIY GUIDE TO MARKETING
for Small Charities and
Voluntary Organisations

Moi Ali

© 1996 Moi Ali.

First published 1996. Reprinted 1997.

Published by the
Directory of Social Change
24 Stephenson Way, London NW1 2DP
Tel: 0171 209 5151, fax: 0171 209 5049
e-mail: info@d-s-c.demon.co.uk
from whom further copies and a publications list
are available.

The Directory of Social Change is a registered
charity No. 800517.

Typeset by Diarmuid Burke.

Printed and bound by Page Bros., Norwich.

British Library Cataloguing-in-Publication Data.
A catalogue record for this book is available
from the British Library.

ISBN: 1 873860 97 8

Other Directory of Social Change departments:
Courses and Conferences tel: 0171 209 4949
Charityfair tel: 0171 209 1015
Charity Centre tel: 0171 209 0902
Research tel: 0171 209 4422

Directory of Social Change Northern Office:
Federation House, Hope St, Liverpool L1 9BW
Courses and Conferences tel: 0151 708 0117
Research tel: 0151 708 0136

ABOUT THE AUTHOR

Moi Ali runs her own PR consultancy, The Pink Anglia Public Relations Company, which specialises in public relations, communications and marketing services for voluntary organisations and the public sector. She has over 12 years' experience in public relations and promotional marketing, working not only for charities and voluntary organisations, but also for PR/marketing consultancies, and in both the public and private sectors.

Moi is the author of *The DIY Guide to Public Relations*, also published by the Directory of Social Change.

CONTENTS

INTRODUCTION

Marketing is considered a serious academic discipline, and many marketing books take this to heart. They are heavy, theoretical and difficult for a lay person to get to grips with. A further problem for charities and voluntary organisations is that most of them are written for businesses or those with an academic interest in marketing; few tackle the issue in a practical way, and fewer still are interested in examining marketing from a charity's unique perspective. This book is refreshing in that it does both these things.

It has been written specially for organisations which are either new to marketing or very inexperienced. Explaining how to do your own marketing on a shoestring, the book also shows how to undertake cost-effective marketing with a larger budget. As the book guides you through the various aspects involved in developing a marketing strategy for your organisation, you can find out how to take an organised and strategic look at what marketing can do for you.

This is a plain English guide; it is as jargon-free as possible, and written in a clear, readable and accessible style. Although it covers marketing theory, it is a very practical book, with plenty of tips and hints to make your marketing task easier. It is, though, a starter book. Marketing is a huge subject and each of the chapters in this book could easily be a book in its own right. The book's aim is to introduce the subject very broadly; readers interested in undertaking a more in-depth study of marketing will need to follow-up by reading further, more detailed marketing texts.

However, particularly for the small or medium sized charity, this book will provide an easily dipped into working manual which readers will find themselves referring to again and again. You may find it useful in conjunction with its companion title, *The DIY Guide to Public Relations*, for a more comprehensive approach to the subject.

WHAT IS MARKETING?

What's in this chapter?

■ *a broad discussion of what marketing is and how it differs from selling.*

■ *arguments for why a marketing approach is vital for today's voluntary sector.*

■ *thoughts on how to get started on the road to becoming a needs-led organisation rather than a resource-driven one.*

As a DIY book, the aim is to be light on theory and heavy on practice. But some theory is inevitable. Without a basic understanding of what marketing means, no voluntary organisation can hope to get it right. That's why this introductory chapter is more discursive and theoretical than the others. It will give you the necessary information base so you can get maximum benefit from the rest of the book. If this section is a bit too heavy for you, bear with it. The following pages really are an important foundation for the subsequent more practical, hands-on chapters.

Let's start with a look at marketing itself. What exactly is it?

WHAT EXACTLY IS MARKETING?

The first thing to understand about marketing is that it is not just another word for selling. If it were, it would be of absolutely zero relevance to the vast majority of voluntary organisations, which neither make nor sell goods. The trouble is that 'marketing' is often used in everyday speech as a synonym for selling and for promotion. We talk about the marketing of a new product, when we really mean its advertising and promotion, which hopefully leads to sales. Sales and promotion are product-led: you start with a product or service which you have to persuade customers to buy. Selling is what happens in charity shops, where there is a supply of goods and you display them in the hope that they will be bought. It is also what happens at jumble sales, bring-and-buy events, bookstalls and so on. Marketing is an altogether more complex beast: it involves both sales and promotion, but a lot more besides.

Don't Confuse Marketing and Selling

Trouble occurs when people confuse selling and marketing, setting out to attract sales before they have even thought about marketing. This was what happened with the famous, some would say infamous, Sinclair C5, the mini car-cum-trike invented by Sir Clive Sinclair and launched in 1985. He came up with a nifty and quirky little invention which, he believed, would revolutionise British motoring. Instead of driving around in cars, we would have these greener, cleaner and cheaper electric powered C5s. The problem was that by starting with a product, he was acting on his hunches and not on objective, research-based facts. Some have made their fortune on a hunch – their 'feel' for something happened to coincide with the rest of the world's – but that's not always so. Take Sir Clive. His idea was fantastic – to him. His enthusiasm was not shared by the rest of us, by his market. His product therefore flopped, he went bankrupt, and now his C5 can only be seen in a motoring museum.

First Establish Needs

So if marketing isn't just about selling, what is it about? Marketing's starting point is to identify (usually using some form of research) customers' needs and wants, and then to develop a product or service that can satisfy those needs. Promotion and sales take place after the development of a product or service based on customers' needs. By finding out what customers want before you develop a product or service, you avoid a potential mismatch between your service and their needs. Had Clive Sinclair gone about it this way, he would probably be a very rich man now.

But what's this got to do with charities and voluntary organisations? Quite a lot. Whether you sell goods (via mail order catalogues or through a charity shop, for example) or whether you run a service or a pressure group, you need to understand and use marketing techniques. Why? To maximise your efficiency and minimise risk. Proper marketing will help you to develop new services that are needed by the community which you serve, and to attract the necessary funding to run them. And it will help you to plan according to actual need, not gut feeling.

A FAIR EXCHANGE

Another important aspect of marketing is that is revolves around an exchange. The customer pays money and in return gets a product or service. Even for charities the concept of exchange is relevant. When a donor makes a donation they get in return a feeling of having helped, a feeling that makes them feel good (or at least, less bad or less guilty).

Making What You Can Sell

Marketing is sometimes defined as 'making what you can sell, not selling what you can make'. Had Clive Sinclair made what he could sell, he would not have made the C5. It is a good motto, but there are charities for whom it does not apply: some campaigning organisations and some health promotion groups, for example. Suppose you are campaigning against racism; your target must surely be racists, for there is no point in preaching to the converted. If you give them what they will readily buy, it certainly won't be anti-racism; quite the opposite, in fact.

It is the same with health promotion. A campaign aimed at getting people to take more exercise, change their diet, give up smoking and reduce alcohol intake is aimed at 'beer 'n' baccy' couch potatoes. They might benefit from acting on your advice, but what do you do if they are not interested? Giving them what they want would involve developing cream cakes that make you slim, pills that replace the need for exercise, and non-carcinogenic cigarettes! Your aim is to get them to do something they probably don't want to do, which on the surface appears the very antithesis of marketing.

While the above examples do not fit neatly into the traditional marketing model, there is still a lot that marketing can do to help. It can help package and present anti-racism or health promotion messages to give them more appeal for the intended audience. It can help charities reach out to their audience. It can help them to understand their audiences' needs. So even in this situation, marketing has a role.

Turning Customers Away

But there is a further problem with the notion that marketing is about selling what you can make. There are often cases when a voluntary organisation is asked to provide a service for which funding is available, but the organisation declines for reasons of principle (something few commercial companies would consider). Let's take an example: suppose that you have been asked by a statutory body to provide a service for older people. The funding on offer is, in your view, inadequate. A service can be provided for that amount, but it would fall far short of the standard that you believe is required. You might therefore decide to turn your customer away because doing business with them would result in:

a) your having to provide a substandard service which would, you believe, cause serious damage to your reputation for providing high quality, innovative services, thus leading to a future loss of credibility.

b) your having to compromise your principles: if you genuinely feel that older people deserve better than this, you would be a hypocrite to provide it.

Clearly in this example, you would be refusing to sell what you could make! There would be nothing to stop you providing the service, except principle, and that's something that is very important to the voluntary sector.

WHY DO CHARITIES NEED MARKETING?

Charities can no longer ignore marketing, if they ever could. Those who do, do so at their peril. Here are three compelling reasons why you cannot afford to ignore marketing:

1. Coping With a Contract Culture

In an increasingly competitive environment, charities and voluntary organisations are having to compete with each other (and sometimes with commercial organisations and the public sector) for their share of funding and donations, or to sell their products or services. They now also have to negotiate contracts with local authorities, health authorities and even with other voluntary organisations. Social work departments and health authorities are increasingly changing from being providers of services to purchasers of services. More and more, the voluntary sector is providing mainstream services that were previously the sole responsibility of local and national government.

Consequently the operating environment for charities is more financially and 'market' driven, and considerably more competitive, than ever before. This is reflected in the language charities now speak: many use business jargon, appoint staff with business degrees or commercial experience, and produce business plans and strategies. But even for very small voluntary organisations, marketing has become a must. A good understanding of their market, and well-researched products and services, can make the difference between survival and extinction. That's a powerful reason for thinking marketing.

> **TRUE STORY**
>
> *The British Heart Foundation had 34 shops in 1989. By January 1996 it had 227, with around 40 new outlets opening each year. It puts its success and growth down to taking a professional approach, applying a commercial discipline, and recruiting store managers from retail backgrounds. It has seen a 96% increase in total income from its shops, sales per shop are up by nearly 50%, and the average profit margin is 27%. If you run a shop, do your figures compare well with these? Do you even know how your shops are doing? If not, read on!*

2. The Packaging of Unpopular Causes

Some voluntary organisations deal with unpopular causes – HIV/AIDS, prostitution, drug misuse, gay issues, to name but a few – and they, too, can benefit from good marketing, which can repackage the cause and present it in a more appealing or popular way. Some would call that 'selling out'; for those of us who live in the real world, it is called survival. If you can present your cause to make it more attractive and inviting, and the result is more and larger donations, support from trusts, and funding from your local authority, surely that's better than taking the moral high ground and ending up as a lost cause?

3. The Meeting of Needs

If the first two reasons have not convinced you that you need to think marketing, this surely will. Marketing as a discipline can help you to identify need and develop solutions to meet a need. Obviously marketing cannot achieve miracles, creating a wonderful world at the mere swish of a magic wand. But it can take you back to basics and ensure that you develop services around the needs of your clients. Over time too many organisations have moved away from being needs-led and have become resource-driven. They are running services tailored to their budget, not the needs of their client group. If you adopt a marketing approach you may discover that you too have done this, and that you need to refocus your attention, listen more to your clients, and redevelop many of your services.

Marketing techniques can help charities to promote their work, to raise money, to develop services that people need and want, and to run successful campaigns on important issues. Put like that, can you afford not to take marketing seriously?

The statutory funding that many charities have relied on over the years is now subject to competition in a way that it simply wasn't in the past. With an increasing number of charities after an ever smaller pot of money, with street-wise funders demanding 'value for money' and 'added value,' and with the move to involving the private sector in many projects, marketing is something that can no longer be avoided.

INTERESTING FACT

The Central Office of Information has one of the largest advertising accounts in the UK, and governments of all political persuasions are major suppliers and users of market research data. In 1990 the government spent £20 million on advertising the electricity privatisation share offers.

CHAPTER TWO

WHO ARE YOUR 'CUSTOMERS' AND HOW CAN YOU KEEP THEM?

What's in this chapter?

- *how to pinpoint and categorise your customers.*
- *how to 'segment' your market.*
- *what your customers expect of you.*
- *why individual and corporate customers buy and what motivates them.*
- *customer care, keeping your customers and dealing with customer complaints.*

Customers are central to successful marketing, so understanding their place in your marketing strategy, and recognising who they are, are the first steps to establishing a programme of marketing activity.

Marketing places customers' needs and wants at the centre. To an extent that's what many charities do anyway, but often for very different reasons. In the old, paternalistic and philanthropic days of the voluntary sector, service-users were expected passively to receive and be grateful. The donors and charity trustees knew best and it never occurred to anyone to ask what the user wanted. They were never consulted about their views on the workhouse or the almshouse. But now that's all changed, in many organisations at least. Part of today's voluntary sector philosophy is about listening to service-users and responding to their needs and wants. It is also about involving them in the development of services and giving them a voice and a part to play in the decision-making process. It is done because it is good practice to run client-centred services. So just as a holiday company finds out what holidays people wish to take, and plans its packages around meeting that desire, so a voluntary sector project for teenagers should find out what they want and then meet the need. But there is a crucial difference in the two approaches which, on the surface, appear similar. In the case of the holiday company the 'service-users' (i.e. holiday-makers) are the customers. In the case of the youth scheme, the users may (indeed, should) be regarded as 'customers' or 'clients', but they are not customers in the true sense of the word. It is the funders i.e. the people who pay for the service, who are the real customers. They are the ones who part with money. When it comes to your marketing, you need to understand that you probably have two (or more) sets of customers: the funders (be they statutory bodies or individual donors) and the service-users.

WHO ARE YOUR CUSTOMERS?

Even for commercial enterprises, defining who your customers are may not be straightforward. Take the case of children's foods such as Postman Pat spaghetti, for example. The food is eaten by children, but it is bought by adults. The adult, therefore, is the customer, even though the promotion of the product is aimed at children. It is the same with the voluntary sector. It is the drug-user who uses the needle exchange, but it is the health authority or NHS trust which is the customer, for they pay the voluntary organisation to run the service. The services of the needle exchange are promoted to drug-users in the same way that the spaghetti is promoted to children. The first lesson in marketing, then, is to recognise the split between the user/consumer of your product or service and the funder/customer.

THE USER/FUNDER CUSTOMER SPLIT

You should regard both your service-user and your service-funder equally as customers; without people to use your service, or without organisations to fund it, there would be no service. Your aim is to develop services that are genuinely needed by your target user group, as well as services that funders want to buy. So you instantly have two very different customers to cater for. Two sets of customers to research. Two lots of customers to promote to. That's what makes your marketing task so much more complex than the average commercial marketing exercise. By the time you have added in the 'political' dimension, which affects the work of many voluntary organisations, you have on your hands a marketing job that requires great skill and understanding if you are to do it successfully.

Many voluntary organisations have three other sets of customers:

1. Supporters/Members

Some organisations rely on income from supporters, whose membership fee helps to pay for the services they run. Take the National Trust, which receives statutory funding, but also has a large membership base which is essential to its work. Its aim is to preserve important buildings and landscape for the nation. Its customers might buy membership to support this vital work, or simply because it gives them free entrance to stately homes. What is clear is that what individual members buy, what they pay and what they get is something different from what the big statutory purchasers are buying when they hand over their money. The government might give £500,000 to a heritage organisation in order to fulfil its governmental duty to preserve the nation's heritage. The member might pay £10 to the same organisation simply to get the free magazine every month.

2. Donors

Those who give to your charity are donors. Some will be individuals, others will be organisations, whether corporate donors, charitable trusts or foundations. They are buying something from you when they send in their cheques. Perhaps giving makes individuals feel better, appeases their guilt, offers an opportunity to do some good in the world, or provides a chance to right an injustice they feel strongly about. For a company, giving could be about buying an enhanced image or being socially responsible. Donors are, for some charities, very important customers. Most charities do not regard donors as a homogeneous group; they realise that the needs, wants and interests of an individual donor are probably different from those of a corporate giver. That's why they segment their donor data base, perhaps even introducing different categories of individual donors (i.e. building up donor profiles).

3. Volunteers

Just as volunteers are generally not considered to be staff, because they do not receive a salary from you, so they are often not seen as customers, for they do not pay for the privilege of helping you. Yet they are customers in the sense that an exchange takes place. You rely on their goodwill to keep your 'business' going, and they get something in return – whether it is work experience, a spiritual gain, something to make them feel useful or a chance to help something they care about. The fact that money is not exchanged doesn't make them any more or any less of a customer.

DIFFERENT EXPECTATIONS

Most charities will probably have individual 'customers' (donors and supporters, for example) as well as service-users, statutory purchasers and corporate donors. It is important to realise that the way organisations (whether corporate or statutory bodies) 'buy' is different to the way individuals buy. The influencing factors are different, the motivation is different, and generally the sums of money involved are very different.

A service-user might use a free alcohol counselling service because they have a drink problem and need help. A health authority might contract a voluntary organisation to run the counselling service because it helps them meet their statutory healthcare objectives. A whisky manufacturer might sponsor the service's promotional leaflet to help it create a socially responsible image. The service-user, the health authority and the whisky company are customers, but the needs, wants and motivations of the individual customer are very different from those of the statutory and corporate ones.

MARKET SEGMENTATION

Once you can recognise the different types of customer you have, you can develop strategies for their different needs and expectations: this is what is known as 'market segmentation'. At the heart of market segmentation is the recognition that you have a range of different customers and that you need to split your market into different segments in order successfully to meet those varying needs. Let's look at an example: a children's hospice charity. It might have the following customers:

- **Individual donors** – their need is to help what they see as a worthwhile cause.

- **Volunteers** – their need is to help in a more practical way, perhaps in the fundraising office, by making goods to sell, or by spreading the word through speaking engagements.

- **Corporate donors** – they wish to help and to be associated with a well regarded and worthwhile charity. They also hope that their association with an important charity will reflect well on them and create goodwill.

- **Health boards/health commissions and social work departments** – they need to buy services for the public they serve. This is their statutory duty.

- **General practitioners** – GPs need to know what services are available for children with life limiting conditions, so that they can make referrals and thus help families.

- **Children with life limiting conditions and their families** – this group needs a place that is a home from home. They may want counselling, support and a listening ear. They also need a fun place to spend time, plenty of activities, good food and comfortable surroundings.

When set out like this it is easy to see what each group might need from the charity. Parents might need to know what to pack for their children, whether special diets can be catered for at the hospice and whether pets can accompany children. Social work departments might need to know full details of the service offered, the costs of the service, and details of the professional qualifications of those providing the service. An individual donor might want to know why their help is needed, how their money will help, and how much of their donation will go in administration.

PINPOINTING THE ORGANISATIONAL CUSTOMER

When you are dealing with an organisation, working out exactly who your customer is requires an understanding of the buying process, with its linked decision-making process. Social work departments 'buy' care in the community services, so they are the customers of voluntary organisations providing these services. But departments are not entities in their own right; they comprise people, some of whom have power and autonomy and others who don't. The customer, then, is not the social work department, but certain key individuals within it. Finding out who your customer is involves asking:

- who decides to buy?

- who are the key decision-makers in the buying/commissioning process?

- how do they arrive at a purchase decision? (by appraising the options in a formal way? by holding a meeting? by using personal contacts?)

- how long is the pre-purchase decision period? (i.e. do they start considering the options six months before a final decision is reached?)

- what are the key dates in the process? (in other words, is there a cut-off date after which they will not, for example, accept applications for funding?)

- at what stage, if any, can you influence the decision?

- who from within influences the decision?

- who makes the final decision?

- how often do they buy? (at the year end? every three years?)

- what do they buy?

In order to answer many of the above questions you need to carry out some marketing research (see Chapter Six).

FOUR WAYS TO GET TO KNOW YOUR CORPORATE CUSTOMERS

Research is essential if you want to get to know your customers better. But without spending too much time or money there are some simple ways of getting to know your organisational customers:

- list the five most important organisations (and people within them) who you need to interview in order to find out what they want from your service/organisation. Go and talk to them.

- list the principal enquiries you want to make with them. Ask about these when you go to see them.

■ list any important magazines or journals that will tell you more about your customers, the issues that concern them etc. Go out and buy them or inspect them in the library.

■ list any exhibitions and events you need to attend which will give you a chance to get to know your customers better. Book tickets and attend them, or exhibit at them.

FINDING YOUR INDIVIDUAL CUSTOMER

Even with individual customers it is not always clear who the real customer is. Let's take the example of a nature/conservation charity specially for young ornithologists. The charity might discover, on carrying out research, that it is adults who buy membership (i.e. take the purchasing decision and pay for the product) even though the charity is aimed at children. It could be that parents regard an interest in ornithology as beneficial for their child's educational and social development. Unlike the Postman Pat spaghetti discussed above, which is bought thanks to the influence of children, this charity's product is bought because adults think it is a good idea, even though it is used by children. While this children's product would be marketed to adults, the spaghetti would be promoted to children, who would then influence parents to buy it. Once you understand the purchasing process, and its influencing factors, you are in a better position to know how, and to whom, you should promote your product.

CATEGORISING YOUR INDIVIDUAL CUSTOMERS

Marketers have over the years developed various ways of categorising customers according to 'type'. Various categories have been suggested, based on social class, occupation, income, and education. The categorisation that is widely accepted is that of the Institute of Practitioners in Advertising, the advertising agencies' professional body. This classification (see below) has been adopted as the standard one by advertisers, marketers, market researchers and a host of others involved in marketing:

AB managerial and professional

C1 supervisory and clerical

C2 skilled manual

DE unskilled manual and unemployed

As with any classification there are problems. When the classification was 'invented', most households were headed by a male 'breadwinner'. It was fairly easy to categorise a family according to his occupation. These days we have many more households comprising two males, or two females, or two equal breadwinners.

Sometimes classification is arrived at by asking people about their income, since there is a correlation between income and occupation. It is possible, though, that two families on the same income will probably have very different interests and lifestyles, depending on their social class and level of education. A middle class family on £20,000 will buy a different newspaper, watch different TV programmes, eat different food and spend spare income in different ways to a working class family on the same income.

You need to be aware of any shortcomings in the classification system you opt for.

WHY BOTHER WITH CLASSIFICATIONS?

It is helpful to categorise customers because it has been proved that groups of customers share characteristics. By understanding the characteristics of particular groups, you can begin to target those groups which are more likely to be disposed towards helping you by donating, or using your service, or supporting your cause.

If you discover that your donors are mainly white, middle-class Guardian readers who give most at Christmas and Easter, you can then target your fundraising appeals by placing adverts in the Guardian at Christmas and Easter. You can also use in your adverts the sort of imagery and text that will appeal to these readers.

In order to segment your market and build up an accurate picture of your many customer types, you will need to undertake research. This can be very basic, simply involving the analysis of information you already have (desk research) or it can be more in-depth, involving your charity in commissioning primary research among your customers. You can read about how to do this in Chapter Six.

WHY DO INDIVIDUALS BUY?

No one buys anything for the sake of it: we buy to fulfil a need. Even the shopaholic who spends money on useless items is buying for a reason, even if the reason is just to satisfy their addiction to shopping! Those of us who give to charity do so because we want to, but why do we want to? Knowing your customer involves first knowing who they are (see above) and second, finding out why they buy. What motivates them? A great deal of work has been done in this area, for obvious reasons. If it were possible to unlock the reasons why people buy, it would give companies a head start in selling. It is, however, impossible to come up with a neat set of reasons why people buy, and when it comes to supporting a charitable organisation, motivations become even more complicated. However, here are a few possibles:

- **need it** – (basic foodstuffs, loo roll, heat and light etc. come into this category). An NHS trust might buy a service from your organisation because they have a responsibility to offer that service, and it is in their interests to provide it via you rather than set up a separate service of their own. In other words, they need it.

- **want it** – (perfumes, alcohol, chocolates and luxury items). Often we buy not from need but from desire. We might not need an Indian wooden box from the Oxfam shop, or a batik bedspread; we buy these things because we like and want them.

- **to make a statement** – sometimes we buy an object because it is a way of making a statement about ourselves. A punk might buy pink hair dye for this reason. That's often why charity merchandise is bought, such as a CND badge, a Save the Whale car sticker, a Greenpeace T-shirt or a 'Rats Have Rights' mug. These items are bought in order to make a statement about us, our moral beliefs or political affiliations. Some of them are practical items, such as the mug or the T-shirt, but we buy them not because we need the object, but because our possession of it says something about us.

- **to re-sell** – wholesalers buy in order to re-sell to retailers, who buy to re-sell to customers. Some charities produce guides and handbooks which others (such as book shops) then buy to re-sell.

- **for entertainment** – (theatre, cinema, horse races, lottery tickets). Tickets to charity balls, charity sporting events, fetes and fairs are bought so the purchaser can enjoy the entertainment (as well as helping the charity).

- **impulse** – often we buy on impulse, particularly when it comes to things we don't particularly need. They catch our eye, they might come in handy later, or they are a bargain. Charity merchandise is often bought for this reason, such as a cheerful Traidcraft waistcoat or some bright Mexican earrings.

- **emotional** – a great deal of charity buying is done for emotional reasons. We buy a second-hand book from a charity shop, or a cake from a fete stall, because we want to help raise money for the cause. That's why we might buy membership of a campaigning organisation. It is also why we send donations to charity. We do it because we care about the issue or subject, whether it is a campaign to expose and stop torture in the Third World or an appeal to build a sanctuary for old donkeys.

Generally people don't buy for just one reason, but for a complex variety of motivations. Someone might buy an enamel CND badge because they are passionately committed to nuclear disarmament, they want to support CND, they want to make a political statement by wearing the badge and because they think it looks stylish and attractive.

You must find out why people buy from you so that you can promote your product effectively. If most of your customers buy your silk blouses because they wish to support the work of the hostel for unmarried mothers in India that made them, your promotional material might read:

> *"Our Delhi Mother and Baby Centre provides a lifeline to unmarried mothers rejected by their families. It offers comfortable rooms, nutritional food for mother and child, a crèche, parenting classes, and provides employment in the community sewing room. That's where these beautiful silk blouses were made. Women from the Delhi Centre make the blouses in return for a decent wage and free lodgings. Our Centre gives them a chance to establish a relationship with their new child, to learn essential parenting skills, and to grow physically healthy. By buying one of their blouses you are helping these women to become self-sufficient and to take care of their child."*

But if your research reveals that people buy the blouses because they are attractive, fashionable and good value, your promotional material would take a very different slant:

> *"Beautiful blouses in the finest silk, the brightest colours, the highest quality but the lowest prices. These stunning silk blouses will not look out of place anywhere – in the office or at a dinner party – nor will they break the bank. And while wearing your blouse you can have the satisfaction of knowing that your purchase has helped single mothers in Delhi ..."*

If you are selling your blouses through wholesalers for re-sale, their motivation is profit. They want to buy cheap and sell dear. To them you might say:

> *"Quality silk blouses in a range of fashionable colours, sizes 10-14. Only £120 per dozen. Will easily retail at £20 plus each."*

There is no need in this case to mention the Delhi Centre. It is irrelevant to the wholesaler, for it is not a motivating factor: re-sale price is the only concern.

To find out why people buy, you need to ask them. There are lots of ways of undertaking research to find out why people buy from you, and some of them are neither costly nor time-consuming. Chapter Six on marketing research looks at how you can carry out this sort of research in-house.

WHY DO ORGANISATIONS BUY?

Individuals buy for a whole set of different reasons. Organisations, though, generally buy in order to fulfil their organisational goals. An individual might give to a mental health charity because they care about the issues surrounding mental health, perhaps because they or a relative have experienced mental health difficulties. A social work department might support a mental health project run by a housing charity because it has a statutory responsibility for the community care of people with mental health problems. In funding the charity it is discharging its duty. But even here the motivation is complicated. One authority might buy services from a particular mental health charity because:

a) it has to provide that service.

b) it is committed to innovation in dealing with people with mental health difficulties, and believes that the particular housing charity has a good track record for innovation.

Another authority might buy into the same service because:

a) it also has a statutory duty to provide that service.

b) it has a policy of supporting local voluntary organisations where possible.

Only by knowing your customers and their motivation can you begin to understand their purchasing decisions. To the first social work department you would need to stress the innovative nature of your work; to the latter you would place more emphasis on being locally-based.

CUSTOMERS HAVE CHOICES

Even when the customer knows what they want to buy, e.g. toilet tissue, they still have choices to make, such as which brand, which colour, recycled or normal, luxury or budget loo roll. Then there's where to buy it. Supermarket or corner shop? And how to pay for it. Cash or (assuming other items are being bought at the same time) cheque, debit, credit or store card.

It is the same when it comes to selecting a charity to give to. We might know that we want a children's charity, but which one? For abused children? Third World children? Deprived children? Physically disabled? Mentally disabled? Disadvantaged? Sick? Holidays for children? Education? Healthcare? Local, national or international? The choice is immense. Then there's how to give. Via a collection can, a legacy, a covenant, a one-off donation, Gift Aid, payroll giving, by volunteering, by buying merchandise, by collecting door-to-door, by organising a fundraising event?

Your aim is to recognise that your customers have choices. You need to understand what those choices are, why they opt for what they do, and how you can persuade more of them to opt for you rather than the competition. There is a paradox, though. For membership organisations (such as the RSPB or National Trust, for example), more customers means more money. By contrast, for service charities more customers i.e. service-users, often means less money. The more service-users a charity has, the more costly the service is to run, often without a concomitant increase in funding. So whereas a commercial body wants to get more customers full stop, service charities need to attract both more customers and more funding.

There is a further paradox when it comes to charities and their customers. Companies try to attract and keep their customers; their survival depends on it. For many charities, however, the philosophy is about decreasing dependence and fostering autonomy. Voluntary organisations working in the field of disability, for example, aim to create a world in which disabled people can be as independent as possible, by removing barriers that prevent them from getting about, working, going on holiday, studying etc. Such an approach, if successful, will put such charities out of business once their mission is achieved. No business would deliberately plan to make itself redundant.

KEEPING CUSTOMERS

It costs seven times as much to attract a new customer as to keep an existing one. It therefore makes great sense for cash-strapped charities to ensure that they have first rate customer care, because good customer care is the best way you have of keeping your customers and, via their word of mouth, attracting new ones.

Some of our more successful companies have achieved their success by caring about their customers and having clear procedures and comprehensive training to ensure that customer care is a reality, not just rhetoric. Many charities are now wising up to customer care. The days are gone when recipients were expected to be both deserving and grateful. Today's customer culture has reached the voluntary sector, and there is a widely held view that customers, whether paying or not, have rights.

Caring about customers, and taking steps to provide them with a top class service (given the limitations that will be imposed on you due to funding restraints) is a natural part of charities' thinking today, although it is rarely approached in an organised way, still less considered as part of a marketing strategy.

Meeting needs also means managing expectations. Customer care involves setting out clearly what your customers need (based on what they tell you, not on what you surmise) and explaining what you can deliver. You must provide a quality service that meets reasonable expectations, and be prepared to take swift remedial action whenever you fail.

FIRST STEPS TOWARDS A CUSTOMER CARE CULTURE

Few people cannot tell stories of poor customer service from their own recent experience. It happens to us all every week – in restaurants, shops, in railway stations and on buses, face to face, over the telephone and in writing. Poor customer service is so common that it is likely that your organisation is as guilty of it as any other.

If you visit a shop and the assistant ignores your obvious need for help because he is too busy telling his colleague about a football match, that gives you a bad impression not only of that shop assistant, but of the store as a whole, and all the other stores in the chain. You judge it all by your one experience of one member of staff. That's how charities are judged too. If one of your staff is rude or unhelpful, that reflects on the rest of you.

Organisations do not exist as entities in their own right. They are made up of staff and judged on the basis of the skills and attitude of those staff. For some of your staff, customer care will be second nature; others will need to learn it. All staff will need to be trained in customer care, and the training programme should form part of your marketing strategy.

If you are an organisation with many functions, you may need to organise a range of different customer care training sessions. For example, customer care training for staff running your mail order catalogue would need to cover different issues to training specially for HQ fundraising staff, or for volunteers who work in your charity shops.

Good customer care can be measured. You can record and evaluate it in an objective way, for example by:

■ timing how long it takes to answer the telephone.

■ timing how long it takes to reply to mail.

■ counting the number of customer complaints.

■ counting the number of complimentary letters you receive.

Based on the raw information you gather about your service and performance, you need to set demanding yet achievable standards (e.g. all calls answered in three rings and put through to the right person first time). It is a good idea to have a customer care working group to examine customer

---

TRUE STORY

A friend of mine called a local Alzheimer's organisation to find out some specific information for his mother, who herself was suffering from the disease. He was told that they would send him some information. Nothing arrived so he called again. A week or so later he received a glossy information pack which did not contain the information he had asked for. He felt that charity was not very well organised, did not listen and did not understand his needs. As a result he changed his mind about leaving them a legacy from his mother's estate, over which he has power of attorney. In this case, good customer care would have paid dividends for the charity concerned. How much goodwill and custom do you miss out on without ever knowing it?

care, to come up with ideas for achieving it, and to set and monitor standards.

Publicise the standards you are aiming for, measure your performance regularly and publish this too. Failure to meet your standards needs to be explained – to other staff and to your customers.

CUSTOMER CHARTERS

The government's Citizen's Charter, Patient's Charter, Tenant's Charter etc. set out clearly what we can expect as consumers of public services. Have you told your clients what they can expect? Better still, have you asked them what they expect? This is what marketing is about.

> **TIP**
> *Make sure that at least one person in your organisation (possibly a voluntary member) is charged with the task of overseeing customer care, even if you are a very small organisation. Make sure that person sees every customer complaint and is informed of the outcome.*

VOLUNTEERS AS CUSTOMERS

As we said above, volunteers are customers too. You should take very special care of them, for they are an extremely valuable asset. The Volunteer Centre UK conducted a survey which revealed that Britain's 22 million volunteers contribute as much as £41 billion a year to GDP (gross domestic product) – more than that produced by the energy, construction or water supply industries! Treat them badly and charities will lose this enormous annual boost. Volunteers can generate income for you (by fundraising for example), they can help preserve your funds (by removing the need to buy in extra help), and they can make otherwise impossibly expensive services (such as a befriending or free counselling service) affordable to operate. So in many ways they are one of your most important customers. Your success certainly depends on them.

Why is it, then, that so many volunteers are treated like 'dogs-bodies' or unpaid skivvies? Too few volunteers are given interesting and rewarding jobs to do. Many are taken for granted. Few are given a contract, training, a job description. It is amazing that so many put up with it! There are, though, some charities who treat their volunteers very well, who appreciate and value their contribution, and who ensure that their work is worthwhile and fulfilling. Are you one of those? If not, you could be losing some very valuable customers.

BUILDING BRAND LOYALTY

Companies spend vast amounts of money trying to ensure that their customers remain loyal. They will only continue 'buying' from you if you treat them well (by getting your customer care right) and offer the right products (which is what marketing is all about). There are things you can do to enhance a customer's loyalty to your cause:

- **thank them** for being customers and show their support is appreciated.

COMPLAINTS FACT FILE

■ *people are generally very reluctant to make formal complaints, but most will grumble to others about poor service.*

■ *of all dissatisfied customers, 96% make no complaint!*

■ *however, they do tell seven others how bad you are.*

■ *13% will tell at least 20 others.*

■ *commercial organisations are more likely to receive complaints because their customers have paid for something and therefore feel that they have more of a right to expect a certain standard.*

■ *charities are less likely to receive complaints: users of their services are vulnerable or would regard a complaint as standing in the way of gratitude.*

■ **keep them** up to date with news and developments.

■ if feasible and appropriate, **give them** loyalty rewards e.g. 10% off their next membership subscription.

COMPLAINTS

Customer care is not about handling complaints, it is about ensuring that you get things right in the first place, thus removing the causes of complaint. Inevitably, though, even in well-run charities things do occasionally go wrong, and you need to be ready to respond properly and to correct errors.

Marketing-led organisations should encourage complaints, not regard them as threats. Complaints are a bit like free research: they can provide you with data on where you are failing, thus enabling you to put it right. To do this you need a system for copying customer complaints to relevant staff, so that there is an opportunity for a complaint to result in a policy or service delivery change or improvement. If your office is inaccessible for people with pushchairs, and no toys are available in your reception area for the many parents who need to bring their children with them, a visit to your office will be an ordeal, even if the service you offer is, in other respects, first class. Perhaps you have failed to notice this shortcoming. A complaint can identify it for you and give you a chance to put it right, thus further improving your service. This will only come about if the person dealing with complaints feeds them through to someone with responsibility for taking corrective action.

CHAPTER THREE

WHAT IS YOUR 'PRODUCT'?

What's in this chapter?

■ *finding out what your product is.*

■ *products within products.*

■ *the organisation as a product and ideas as products.*

■ *the options for developing new products and expanding into new markets.*

■ *how incentives, endorsements and testimonials can help you 'sell' your product or service.*

What is your product? Ask any manufacturer and they could answer without hesitation, but it may not always be obvious for many charities. In conventional marketing a product is the thing you produce in order to sell. Some charities sell goods proper – such as gifts and Christmas cards via mail order catalogues, or aids for disabled people, or second-hand clothes through charity shops.

The majority of Britain's top 200 charities trade, with more than half of them having a separate trading company. But what is their product? They probably have a range which encompasses far more than they sell in their shops or through their catalogues. In the case of charity shops, why do charities run them? Usually as a means of raising funds for their 'real' work, such as medical research (a cancer charity), aid (a third world charity), campaigning (a pressure group), to fund a service (a cats' home) or whatever. Let's look at the cancer charity. It might run shops in order to raise funds to:

■ research the causes of cancer and look for cures.

■ provide hospices for terminal cancer patients.

■ provide support and counselling to families of cancer sufferers, both during their illness and after their death.

The charity could, therefore, be said to have four products: the goods sold in the shops and the three services above. It needs to develop and promote each separately, and yet each needs to be linked as part of an integrated marketing strategy. There's no point in appointing new medical researchers and opening new hospices if the shops are bringing in too little income to support these. The success of one product often depends on the success of another – very profitable shops might enable the charity to open another hospice or to undertake new research.

It is really important that you itemise each of your products. That way you can measure the effectiveness and performance of each, and develop separate promotional programmes. If one product is clearly in difficulty, you can take action to ensure that it does not pull other products (or indeed the whole organisation) down with it. Even charities involved in just one line of 'business' will probably have a range of different products. A charity for elderly people might have:

- residential homes.

- a befriending and visiting service.

- a day centre.

- a meals on wheels service.

- a publications division producing good practice guides for professionals who work with elderly people.

- an information division producing advice for old people on how to guard against crime, keep warm in winter and keep fit in old age.

- a training division running courses for professionals who work with older people.

- a campaigning wing lobbying for improved rights for older people.

All of the above relate to older people, and yet clearly they are very separate and distinct products, each requiring a very different marketing approach. Some are free services, some attract a fee. Some are aimed at old people, others at professionals. That's why it is so important to start listing, so that you can see how diverse your work is, even if as an organisation you have a very integrated feel. So sit down now and list all of your products. Do you currently treat each as a separate product? Is each one promoted, costed and evaluated separately? Do you run one product at a profit in order to subsidise a less profitable (or even loss making) but nevertheless much-needed service? Are you clear that this is what you are doing?

Many companies employ 'product managers' to oversee the development and promotion of individual products. For example, a bank might have a VISA product manager, one for current accounts, one for business borrowing, one for mortgages and one for savings accounts. Although banks are in the business of borrowing and lending, each of its products has an individual role to play within that.

PRODUCTS WITHIN A PRODUCT

Look at the fictitious example above of the charity for the elderly. One of its services is an information division. Presumably this division will itself produce a range of products, such as:

- a Freephone information hotline.

- a 'Keep Fit in Old Age' diet and exercise pack.

- a home security leaflet and video.

- cut price home insulation products.

You need to remember, when listing your products, to itemise the products produced by each of your services.

WHEN YOU ARE THE PRODUCT

Sometimes, one of the products an organisation sells is itself, or its reputation. For example, the Vegetarian Society sells its logo to food manufacturers, who use it to endorse their products and verify their non-animal composition. Companies buying this are not paying for the privilege of using someone else's logo on their products, they are paying for the beneficial associations they will get from their relationship with a respected vegetarian organisation.

The Plain English Campaign sell their 'Crystal Mark' in very much the same way. Organisations wishing to use the Crystal Mark logo must first show that the material on which they plan to use it is indeed plain English. They must also pay a fee.

Another charity, the RSPCA, markets itself as a product, as you can see from the following excerpt from one of their ads, which was placed in Marketing, a weekly newspaper for marketing professionals. It reads:

> *"HOW THE RSPCA CAN HELP YOUR COMPANY BECOME A TOP DOG*
> *We'd like to offer you another way of looking at the RSPCA. We may be a charity but we're also a big business opportunity. We have one of the highest spontaneous awareness measurements of any charity in the UK and constantly feature among the top UK organisations in the news. With so much public support for our work the RSPCA makes an ideal business partner. As over half the households in Britain own pets, building a relationship with us could help raise your company's profile, increase sales and present a positive image, as well as helping us in our lifesaving work. Such a relationship certainly worked with White Horse Whisky, Superdrug, Burmah and Kellogg's..."*

Interestingly, the RSPCA use endorsements in their advert (see below). By naming big companies they have worked with, they provide reassurance to readers that their product must be good – otherwise the household names quoted would not have bought it. This technique is also used in a Red Cross promotional advert:

> *"... This year, with the help of such famous names as Zeneca, Barclays Bank, British Telecom, Somerfield Stores*

and Selfridges, we have raised hundreds of thousands of pounds, while our corporate sponsors have enjoyed the benefits of supporting the British Red Cross ..."

AN IDEA AS A PRODUCT

For many voluntary organisations and pressure groups, their product is an idea – such as anti-racism, or safe sex. Even ideas can benefit from being marketed properly. The same principles apply. You need to think about your product – the idea. You need to consider its promotion – via editorial coverage, perhaps, and campaign leaflets. You must think about place – how people can get to hear about your idea. And you need to consider price. Even ideas have a price. For example, if your 'idea product' is that nobody should live in poverty in Britain, a cost will be attached to putting your idea into practice. The cost to the taxpayer would probably be enormous in terms of increasing benefits etc. That is what is known as the 'impact cost'. If you are to stand any chance in selling any product, the price must be right. For campaigning organisations and others selling ideas, your impact cost must be considered as part of your own marketing work.

THE IDEA BEYOND THE PRODUCT

So far I have looked at products (physical products as well as services) and at ideas as products. There's another consideration: the idea behind your product. For example, a cosmetics manufacturer should see its products as lipstick, mascara etc. But they should also realise that their 'generic product' is beauty (or the hope of beauty). A washing powder manufacturer sells cleanliness, not soap powder. What is the idea behind your product? If you provide supported accommodation for people leaving psychiatric hospitals, you are not just providing a community care service: you are offering hope, independence and freedom to your clients. Look behind your products and see what you are really selling.

GOING FOR GROWTH

The aim of most companies is to grow and, through growth, to prosper. Some charities regard this as inappropriate behaviour for the voluntary sector. Growth is equated with empire-building, predatory and aggressive actions, counter to the spirit of co-operation that is believed to exist within the sector. It need not be like this. It is possible to expand and to build up a solid base without treading on toes or invading a fellow charity's patch. When it comes to growth, charities have available to them the same options as companies. They can go for:

- **market penetration** – this is where you take your existing products to your existing markets. Your aim is to capture a bigger share of this market, or to reach previously unreached potential customers.

- **market development** – Here you take your existing products, but you promote them to new target markets.
- **product development** – this is where you develop brand new products, but offer them to your existing target markets.
- **diversification** – this involves complete change. You are developing new products and offering them to new markets, a risky strategy for charities and businesses alike.

The low risk option for charities is to aim for **market penetration**. You do not have to develop new products or find new markets, all you need to is ensure that you penetrate your existing market. Of course that's easier said than done. Suppose your market is elderly wealthy women who, by and large, are the main group to leave you legacies. To penetrate the market you need to reach all the wealthy elderly women who currently have made no provision for you in their will. You can see the problem immediately. How do you know who they are? How do you reach them? There is no easy answer, though you can read more about targeting your key audiences later on in the book.

Market development involves taking your existing products to new markets. It might be that you run a confidential telephone counselling service for teenagers in Manchester. You could develop your market by offering the same service, but to teenagers in Bolton, Bury and Rochdale.

If you wanted to aim for a strategy of **product development**, you would need to find some new products for your existing market. Remember that marketing is not about making what you think people need, it is about finding out what people need (by asking them) and then developing the products and services that will meet that need. If you discover that the blind people for whom you run a drop-in centre have difficulties getting their weekly shopping, you might decide to develop a service to meet that need.

Diversification as a means to growth is risky. For many charities it may also be illegal, depending on what your constitution says about your aims as an organisation. Certainly for charities reading this book – those new to marketing – it is not an advisable route.

GIVE AN INCENTIVE

Whether you want to grow by reaching new markets or penetrating an existing one, you may want to use 'incentives' to help encourage take up of your product. An incentive is something additional to the product that is offered as an inducement. For example, a bank might offer a free travel plug for anyone buying over £500 worth of travellers' cheques. An environmental charity might offer a free address book made from recycled, chlorine-free paper to new members. If you are considering offering an incentive, ask yourself:

- ■ what incentive would we offer?
- ■ what would the cost be?
- ■ is the incentive appropriate?
- ■ is it likely to boost sales?
- ■ would it boost sales by enough to cover the cost of the incentive?
- ■ how do we know? on what evidence are we basing our assumptions?

DON'T BRIBE, INCENTIVISE!

It can be difficult getting incentives right, especially for charities.

- ✗ **don't** come across as trying to bribe customers. They will resent it.
- ✔ **do** offer something appropriate, that links with your work and your members/customers' interests.
- ✗ **don't** appear lavish or wasteful.
- ✔ **do** offer something that will be valued (without appearing extravagant).

> **TRUE STORY**
>
> *A bank was promoting motor loans in July, timed to coincide with the annual spate of new car buying. It decided to offer an incentive that was linked with motoring, and opted for snow shovels. Unfortunately snow shovels were far from motorists' minds, as Britain basked in one of the hottest summers for years. The incentive campaign was a flop!*

If you are planning on using incentives, you need to work out your figures very carefully. There is no point in spending money on incentives if you do not attract enough extra 'business' as a result. But how do you know what effect an incentive will have? The only reliable way is to offer an incentive to one group but not to another similar group. Measure take-up and see if the group offered the incentive was significantly more responsive than the control group. The easiest way to do this is to split your mailing list (see Chapter Ten on direct mail to find out more about 'test mailings'). You can also use questionnaires to find out whether an incentive is likely to affect whether someone joins you/buys from you/supports you. Another purpose is to assess the popularity of different incentive options too.

Charities might use incentives to:

- ■ **persuade people to buy from you rather than a competitor**: for example, if you are selling Christmas cards (along with thousands of other charities) you might want to offer a free pack of gift tags with every box of cards bought.

This might tip the balance in your favour, and persuade them to buy their cards from you rather than from another charity.

- **get people to respond**: if you offer potential members a free gift, but only if they join before a certain deadline, this could prod people into action.

- **get people to buy more of your product**: if you offer an incentive for sales over a certain number, this can encourage people to buy more than they might otherwise do. For example, offering mail order customers free postage on orders over £30 might be enough to persuade some to increase the total of their purchases.

It is not just charities selling goods that can benefit from using incentives. Service charities can also use incentives to advantage. For example, a drop-in centre for single parents might offer free face painting, a free crèche and free coffee and cakes, as an inducement to get parents through the door.

THUMBS UP TO ENDORSEMENTS

Just as some food manufacturers use the Vegetarian Society logo (see above) to endorse their product with the hope of boosting sales, so you may be able to make effective use of endorsements to enhance your products. A certain pet food manufacturer says that it makes the dog food that top breeders recommend. This makes buyers feel reassured of the quality of the product. What can you use to endorse your products?

TESTING OUT TESTIMONIALS

An alternative to an endorsement is the testimonial. With an endorsement, you don't need to use a real person. For example, you could describe a resort as the place travel agents take their holidays. With a testimonial, you need to quote someone's words. Some companies use famous faces to provide testimonials. You don't need to. The words of ordinary people can be every bit as powerful, as the following fictitious example shows: "I was at rock bottom and could see no reason for continuing to live. I felt worthless, unloved and unwanted. Yet with the help of Listening Ear I have turned my life around and made it worthwhile. I now have a wonderful husband and beautiful children, a job I enjoy and a home I am proud of. I owe it all to Listening Ear. They gave me the will to live, helped me sort out my problems and adopt a positive approach. Without their help I dread to think where I would be now."

> **TRUE STORY**
> The following was printed on the envelope of a direct mail appeal: "When my mum was dying of cancer, I had to cope on my own – I support Marie Curie Cancer Care so others don't have to do the same." Alongside the quote was a photograph of a woman; her name; and wording telling us that she has been a supporter of the charity for over ten years. It was a personal touch that was far more powerful than the words of one of the charity officers urging people to help. It was a direct appeal from one individual to another.

> **TIP**
> Use hand-written testimonials, to add authenticity. Also, if the author consents, use their name and a photograph too.

CHAPTER FOUR

WHAT IS YOUR MARKET?

What's in this chapter?

■ *how to get to know your market.*
■ *how to suss out the competition.*
■ *uncontrollable factors that can affect your market.*

One of the key aspects to knowing your market is, as we saw in Chapter Two, knowing who your customer is. But you must also know what you are up against, and in particular, who the competition is. It may all sound a bit too cut and thrust, and rather unseemly, for the voluntary sector. In an ideal world charities would work together in full co-operation and harmony. Or, more likely, there would be no need for charities at all in Utopia. But the reality is that it is a hard world out there. Other organisations are competing against you – for funding, for donations, for sales, even for staff and volunteers. Some charities will survive, they may even grow and thrive, but others will shrink or even die. Those in the latter category are likely to be the ones who refused to consider marketing. Where do you want your organisation to be in five years' time? Dead, buried and long since forgotten? Or going from strength to strength, focused, successful and expanding?

The charities likely to succeed in the fierce outside world are the streetwise ones, those who understand the market and know how to sell themselves as well as their products and services. To know your market you must get to know who your competitors are, then you need to develop a competitive edge, so that you are better, and are seen to be better, than the competition.

WHO ARE YOUR COMPETITORS?

Working out who your competitors are is not necessarily an easy thing to do. Suppose you run an employment scheme for blind people, which involves making wicker baskets which are then sold through local shops in order to help fund the scheme. Projects of this sort are generally not run like a mainstream business; the prices you would need to charge for your products in order to cover your overheads would price you out of the market. So such projects require external funding to act as a subsidy, unlike a commercial set-up making similar products. In a very narrow sense your competitors are those other manufacturers who make products similar to your own, and sell them through similar outlets. But that's only part of the story. If there is a charitable project on the other side of town employing people with various disabilities, including blind people, you might regard them as the competition, particularly if they are funded/subsidised by the same charitable trust or local authority. They are indeed your competitor, but so too are the many other organisations funded by that trust or council, for all are seeking funding from the same finite pot of money. If you regard your competition in too narrow a way, you may lose out.

Geographic or Generic?

Remember that competition can be geographic e.g. a children's charity might be a competitor of a wildlife charity in that both apply to and rely on the same local authority for their funding. But it can also be generic, with national children's charities up against other each other, or national wildlife charities competing with local wildlife charities for the same supporters.

As you can see from the examples above, competition in the voluntary sector is a funny business. Disability charity A is not competing with Disability charity B in the same way as Widget Factory A would be up against Widget Factory B. Chances are that the two factories would be busy chasing the same customers. In the case of the two charities, there would probably be more than enough 'user customers' for both charities. What they would be short on is someone to pay for their services, so their area of competition would not so much be to attract more users, as to attract more funding.

Warning

Some words of warning on the subject of competitors: be careful not to see competition where it does not exist, otherwise you risk becoming paranoid. Some charities are so pre-occupied with so-called competitors that they spend too much time on warfare and not enough on their raison d'être. They are the organisations which do less well in the end.

Once you have worked out who your competitors are, you must monitor them. In the more aggressive world of business, monitoring the competition has been known to involve bugging the boardroom, infiltrating the organisa-

TRUE STORY

I saw an advertisement in a housing association magazine for a firm of designers specialising in housing association annual reports. My own company writes reports for housing associations, but as I do not have an in-house designer I need to buy-in the design work. I called the company to get some information on them, with the intention of commissioning them if I liked their work. I had two reports on the go, needed a designer and was eager to try someone new. The person I spoke to was immediately suspicious of me, and let it show. He regarded me as a competitor, when in reality I was a customer: I wanted to buy his services, not steal his customers. Rather than me asking him about his work, he interrogated me about my motivation in calling him. Eventually I issued an ultimatum: send me some information and I will consider giving you some business, or ignore my request and lose out on some well-paid work. I never heard from the company again. Now they have lost out on a great deal of work, and all because they feared competition where none existed.

tion, even industrial theft and espionage. We're talking here about something altogether more humdrum and definitely more legal.

Six Ways to Keep Your Eye on the Competition

You can monitor the competition by:

1. **talking to them** – finding out from the horse's mouth what they are up to, what the new developments are, whether any plans are afoot. Naturally you may find that in areas of real competition they will not be very forthcoming. But by having some kind of ongoing dialogue with potential competitors, at least you are in touch, you are not isolated from what else is happening, and you have some feel for what is taking place. Remember, though, that just as you are monitoring them, so they too are probably monitoring you.

2. **talking to their users and/or supporters** – sometimes it is possible to find out quite a lot about the competition from those who use or support it. Talking to NSPCC supporters, for example, about why they opt for that charity rather than another children's one, can be very helpful in providing you with the information you need to shape your own charity. It is, of course, not always easy, possible or, indeed, ethical to do this. However, it can be beneficial.

3. **visiting charity exhibitions such as Charityfair** – this is an excellent way of keeping in touch with developments in your field and of finding out what else is happening nationwide. It is a chance to suss out the competition, but also to forge partnerships and to take forward joint initiatives (which is another important element of marketing).

4. **monitoring local and charity/specialist press** – charities like to promote what they are doing, so building up a file of press cuttings is a good way of knowing what a particular charity, or a particular sector, has been doing over the months and years.

5. **monitoring their advertising** – this is particularly important with the charities that attract the bulk of their donations from advertising. Your own adverts will probably be placed in the same publications, so you must know what you are up against. It is also useful to see where other charities advertise. It might be in publications you would not have expected, and that in itself could be useful marketing intelligence. What imagery are your competitors using in their advertising, what messages are they promoting, what line are they taking?

6. **collecting their literature** (annual reports, leaflets, brochures) – to find out what they are doing that you are not. It is also

useful to see what sort of image they are putting across via their publications.

Essentially you want to know what the competition is doing. What is their 'marketing mix'? In other words, what is their product; how do they promote it; what is it sold for and to whom; how do they get customers to the product? Answer these questions and you will have a very clear idea of your competition. Try also to discover their approach and philosophy, find out more about their staff, the conditions under which they run their service, the resources they have available, and anything else you can find out.

Knowing the competition is just one aspect of knowing your market. It also involves developing a really good understanding of your customers, how they think, what their motivation is, what their expectations are, how they regard your organisation etc. Finding out about your market can be costly. Some companies spend huge sums and employ external consultancies to do the research and monitoring. It can be done in-house, though you will need to make the time and space to do it.

You can find out about your market by:

- **talking to your own users/clients** – conduct individual and group interviews to find out what they want from your organisation and your services.

- **talking to those who buy your service** (such as social work departments and health authorities) to establish their reaction to your service, to find out what they think about your strengths and weaknesses.

- **talking to your supporters, members, volunteers and donors** about why they are involved in your work, what they get out of it etc.

- **monitoring competitors** – (see above).

- **monitoring trends** in your market to spot changes in requirements e.g. if you provide residential care for people with learning disabilities, but you failed to react to community care legislation, you will be left with a product that the statutory sector do not want to buy – you will need to develop new products/services – such as community-based support – or you will go out of business.

THE UNCONTROLLABLES

There are always things that will affect your market and the environment in which you work, many of which will be beyond your control. Some will represent a threat to you, while others will offer opportunities, as long as you have an eye on the market, are flexible and ready to adapt to changing environments and changing needs. Some of the uncontrollables you may face include:

Technology

Changes in technology have been vast and rapid. The invention and cheap mass production of the silicon chip has revolutionised our lives. Many of us now have computers at home, and it is possible to store in one small object the size of a calculator information that previously would have occupied a machine the size of a house. Microwave ovens have changed the way we eat (as well as providing new opportunities for 'ready meal' manufacturers), and faxes and mobile phones have altered how we communicate and how our organisations are run. Everything is now so much more instant. There are new technology implications for voluntary organisations, too, and not just in terms of the impact of new products (such as CD ROMs) on how the office is run. There are potentially big implications for some services too. It may be, for example, that the on-line home shopping revolution will mean that disabled people prefer to shop from the comfort of their armchair, thus making your Dial-A-Ride service redundant and causing you to rethink the needs of your customers. (Such a technological change could result in disabled people becoming socially isolated and more housebound than ever; research would uncover this and you could develop new services to address this problem!) We already have the technology to programme a computer to switch off lights, turn on the heating, close the curtains etc. This technology, put to use in the home of a physically disabled person, or someone with dementia, for example, could alter the way you support such people in their homes. It could also have major implications for your funding, if you are having to install expensive hardware in people's homes.

Government policy and laws

The government's care in the community policy has meant the closure of many voluntary sector hospitals and other long-stay institutions for people with learning disabilities and mental health difficulties. It has also opened up new markets for housing providers who can also provide care. Government policy can have the effect of putting some voluntary organisations out of business, while at the same time boosting the work of others. Keeping a close eye on policy developments, and their potential impact on your organisation, is vital if you don't want to be left behind as your competitors move swiftly to adapt to change and to grasp emerging opportunities.

Legislation, too, can create new openings for charities. For example, if drugs were legalised, there might be a need for the establishment of services to respond to this move, perhaps by explaining the pros and cons of certain substances, and by providing public health information and training. If brothels were legalised, it might be necessary to set up health promotion and anti-AIDS initiatives for prostitutes and clients.

When legislation was introduced to enable the government to launch a national lottery, few charities anticipated the effect a lottery and instant scratch cards would have on their fundraising. Charities running their own lotteries or scratch cards – such as Arthritis Care – have been particularly hard hit. A survey by NCVO showed that the proportion of the population giving to charity fell by 14% in June 1995 against the average for June 1993 and June 1992. The lottery has been blamed for this fall. Yet few charities had taken action to find other sources of finance in the period between lottery announcement and launch. Long-term drops in revenue are also expected. Legacies often follow an on-going relationship with a charity; there is a fear that if people are diverting their money from charities to the Lottery, fewer relationships will develop and charities will see a drop in legacy income. Have you considered if this will affect you? Have you taken any steps to manage the situation? Monitoring the situation and anticipating change is an important part of marketing. If you wait until the impact of new legislation is felt before you act, you've waited too long.

Competitors' activities

In business the threat of new competition is always there. Even the former state monopolies now face competition. It is the same in the voluntary sector. There are other organisations out there who are doing similar work, or who also specialise in your field. If one of them comes along and sets up a service in direct competition with yours, which is always a possibility, that will affect your funding and threaten your service. Increasingly, competition is coming from the private and public sectors, as competitive tendering for services grows. You might find yourself competing with brand new competition from these sectors.

Culture and taste/trends

Our growing interest in green issues and our concerns about global warming, CFCs, environmental pollution and so on have had a marked effect on the types of product we now see on our supermarket shelves. (This interest can be traced to the successful work by campaigning organisations such as Friends of the Earth and Greenpeace in encouraging our interest in the planet.) Ten years ago it was necessary to go to a specialist retailer for recycled loo roll, vegetarian food ingredients and environmentally friendly cleaning materials. Now these things are available on every supermarket shelf, and brand new products have been developed too, such as CFC-free aerosols and mass produced vegetarian ready-meals. Commerce spotted a growing trend and created products that satisfied our need to be ethical and green. Even the financial institutions responded by creating ethical investments and other 'green' financial products. Trends can also present charities and voluntary organisations with new marketing opportunities. Campaigning organisations can tap into the public's interest in a particular issue and meet their need to take some kind of action.

Successful marketing depends on knowing your market, having a very clear picture of the competition and what they are up to, and keeping an eye out for the uncontrollables. It also relies on your ability to respond to the uncontrollables by seizing opportunities and anticipating threats. Do all this and you will be better placed to cope with the difficulties the market place throws at you.

CHAPTER FIVE

HOW TO DEVELOP A COMPETITIVE EDGE

What's in this chapter?

■ *how to develop a competitive edge.*

■ *the dangers of price as your competitive edge.*

■ *how to stand out from the competition.*

■ *how to find out if you have a 'unique selling point'.*

Few companies have a queue of people banging at their door to buy their products or services. Most charities don't have hordes of wealthy donors throwing cash at them. It can be hard to attract customers (or supporters) and the ever-growing competition compounds the difficulty. So whether you are a business or a voluntary organisation, you need to demonstrate that you deserve support/custom more than your competitors. You need to show that you are in some way different from the rest. In short you need to achieve a competitive edge if you are to survive and grow. Success depends on:

a) being better than your competitors.

b) knowing how to promote your competitive edge.

BEING BETTER

Being better than others is what the competitive edge is all about. While there are good and bad charities and voluntary organisations, the mass of them fall within the average category. If you are in that category (you probably are) you need to identify or develop something that differentiates you from the others – you need a competitive edge. Your growth (or even your very survival) may depend on your ability to stand out from the crowd. This involves developing something that is recognised and valued by the customer. This might include:

1. Quality of Service

Quality of service is a feature which many companies use to differentiate them from their competitors. Marks and Spencer, or Harrods, for example, use this as a selling point – and clearly it works. It is, though, important to ensure that quality claims are matched by reality: if people's expectations are raised by claims of fantastic quality, and then dashed by their experience of your service, in the long-run you will lose.

Some charities, particularly the smaller ones, are able to offer a higher quality of service. This is because everyone is much closer to that service in a smaller organisation. It is likely to be your only service, and therefore more important to you than if it were just one of many. The quality service that you can offer should be used as a selling point to give you a competitive edge over some of the bigger name charities who might otherwise have a head start when it comes to attracting funding.

2. Flexibility

Small charities are often pitched against the bigger ones when it comes to attracting funding for projects. Without the resources of a big organisation behind you, it can be difficult to promote yourself in a way that will attract the interest and attention of funders. Use your size as a strength, not a weakness. Let it give you the competitive edge. Smaller charities can often be more flexible than larger ones, with less bureaucracy to deal with. They can also be more responsive to changing needs.

3. Personal Service

Smaller organisations generally offer a more personal service. The director of a small social centre for older people is far more likely to know what is happening there than the director of a major national charity specialising in running centres for older people. Use this to your advantage.

4. Value for Money

Even though administration is an essential part of the effective functioning of any organisation, many donors hate the idea of their cash being used in this way. They want it to go straight to 'the cause'. Some charities spend very little on administration, and can use this as their competitive edge – "98p of every pound goes straight to helping Romanian orphans" might be a line that has appeal for potential donors.

5. Charity Image

Image is a powerful source of competitive advantage, and the larger charities with professional PR, design and advertising help find it easier to establish and maintain a good image and a high profile. But even small charities can work on developing and promoting a good image that will help them stand out from the crowd. You can present your image through advertising (for donors, staff, volunteers etc.), publications (such as leaflets and your annual report), and through using the media to gain editorial coverage (by sending news releases or talking to news and feature editors). Remember, though, that a genuine competitive edge involves not just promoting a positive image, but ensuring that your services and products live up to that image.

Assuming that your competition comprises charities offering the same or a similar service to you, you need to come across as (and indeed to be) better. Perhaps you already have a competitive edge but don't recognise it and therefore cannot promote it. To find out if you have an edge that you don't yet know about, start by asking:

- is there anything that we do that is different to/better than our competitors? (e.g. perhaps you train all your staff in customer care or disability awareness).

- what's in it for the customer who buys our products/services? (do they get a friendlier welcome, a lower price, a better deal?).

- what's the gain for them?

- are we less bureaucratic?

- are we more organised?

- are we more client-centred?

- is our service better? How?

- do we represent better value for money? How?

- are we more accountable? How?

> **TRUE STORY**
>
> *A famous baked beans company promoted itself as having a family image, which helped its brand develop a competitive edge. However, when parents wrote to the company for information to help their children with school projects, many never received replies. This was uncovered when a major piece of independent research was commissioned to expose the gap between organisations' image and reality: the company received bad press as a result. The family friendly image that was promoted differed from the reality. Proper marketing involves getting both the image and the reality right.*

FIND AND USE YOUR USP

Your competitive edge might incorporate a USP (see above). That's the thing that differentiates you, making your product or service unique. You might run the only home for legless dogs in the whole of Britain. Or the largest recycling charity in Coventry. Or the oldest established children's charity. Or Britain's first cats' home. Or the only organisation to care for whole families in sex abuse cases. Companies work hard at developing a USP (or several USPs) and then heavily promote them or build brands around them.

Not every charity will have a USP, but if you do, use it to your advantage by making it work for you. To find out if you have a USP, answer the following questions:

- are you the oldest (locally, nationally, internationally)?

- are you the newest?

- are you the largest?

- are you the most cost-effective?

- are you the only one providing that service or product?

- are you the only one providing it locally?

- ■ are you the only one campaigning on that particular issue?
- ■ is there something about your approach that is pioneering or unique?
- ■ were you the first to introduce something that is now commonplace?
- ■ do members get something from you that they do not get with similar organisations? (e.g. a newsletter, monthly updates or a free badge).

Remember that a USP must be meaningful to your customers. You may have several USPs: one that appeals to volunteers, one for corporate donors and one for users. For example:

Volunteers

Enviro-parc is the only environmental charity in Tricester to offer volunteers accredited work experience and full expenses.

Corporate donors

Enviro-parc is the longest established environmental charity in the county; this offers companies a unique opportunity to improve the local environment.

Service-users

Enviro-parc is the largest supplier of environmental cleaning services, with a large team of skilled volunteers available at 24-hours' notice to clean up derelict land, overgrown parks and gardens, littered streets and other environmental eyesores. We are the only organisation working for the public sector, business and the community.

PRICE AS YOUR COMPETITIVE EDGE

In retailing, price is often the determinant factor. Shoppers want bargains, so the shop offering the best price will have the competitive edge. Sometimes charities find themselves forced to compete on price when it comes to achieving funding for services. The commercial practice of tendering for services is now widespread in the public sector, and many charities have to bid to provide a service. As with retailers (many of which have gone out of business as a result of price wars) so too with charities, price-cutting can be a dangerous route to take. Often it will cost you the same to run a service as it will cost another charity; if you offer to do it for less, that means cutting corners and providing an inferior service, which will disadvantage your users. Given that you were set up to help them in the first place, such a move could be regarded as counter-productive. There are, of course, occasions when you can provide the same service for less, because you operate in a more efficient way. Offering to do it for less is legitimate in such circumstances. You are merely making better use of scarce public money.

On the subject of price, while you don't want to offer cut-price, inferior services, you also have to be careful not to price things too high. If the sort of children's crèche you would ideally like to run costs £100 per week per child, but your local authority can only afford to pay £70, you will need to amend/alter your service (in a way that is acceptable both to you and to them) if you are to achieve your funding. If you find that amending your service (and therefore lowering standards or services) is unacceptable to your organisation, you need either to find a new customer who is willing to pay what you wish to charge, or find a new product that will appeal to your existing customers. Alternatively you will need to come up with some other way around the problem, such as grant aid subsidy to make up for the shortfall between what the council can afford and what the service costs. Marketing decisions often involve a trade-off between minimising costs and maximising service and customer satisfaction.

PROMOTE BENEFITS, NOT FEATURES

As stated at the beginning of the chapter, success depends on being better than your competitors (having a competitive edge) and knowing how to promote this. One major mistake that companies make when it comes to promoting their competitive edge is to focus on the features that differentiate their product rather than on the benefits for the customer of the features. For example, a toaster manufacturer might say "Buy this toaster. It boasts a host a unique features including thermal regulator and intelligent eject sensor." That would be promoting features, but customers want to know the benefits. Focusing on benefits, the text would read: "Never again will you have to eat burnt toast. This toaster is able to sense when your toast is done to a turn, and will pop it out and straight onto your waiting plate. So take the hassle out of making breakfast, and never again waste a slice of bread."

Customers want to know what the product will do for them, not what its features are. That also goes for your funders. They want to know that your service will help them make the most effective use of their budget, enable them to meet their statutory duties, and help them to fulfil their commitment to implementing their care in the community strategy on time. That's the benefit to them.

Donors don't want to know about the features of your service, they want to know the benefits. "Your money can save the life of Pramilla and other children like her" (benefits) is better than: "We have a team of fully qualified doctors on the scene in the Third World administering vital vaccinations to children" (features of your service).

PROMOTING YOUR EDGE

Once you have developed a competitive edge, which may include a USP, you need to ensure that it is actively promoted. So many

TRUE STORY

I once did some work for a voluntary housing organisation that was a true pioneer, having been the first to introduce no less than half a dozen new ideas into the world of housing. But it hid its light under a bushel. I discovered these 'firsts' not from the organisation's literature, but from its archives. It was not using them to differentiate it from other housing organisations, or to create a pioneering and innovative image, which would have helped it attract funds. It is not enough to know that you are good at something – shout it so everyone else knows too.

organisations have done wonderful work that really sets them apart from the rest, but it has never occurred to them to promote it. There is no room for modesty. If you've done something that makes you stand out, blow your own trumpet, because you can be sure that your competitors will not blow it for you.

You can promote your competitive edge in all sorts of different ways. The chapters on promotion will give you some ideas.

CHAPTER SIX

MARKETING RESEARCH

What's in this chapter?

■ *the uses to which research can be put.*

■ *how to do your own marketing research.*

■ *how to design a questionnaire.*

■ *the pros and cons of different survey methods.*

■ *how to select a market research consultancy.*

■ *how to use marketing research findings.*

If the mention of 'market research' conjures up images of people standing on the High Street with clipboards, think again. Marketing research is an important tool for voluntary organisations, and some charities spend six figure sums annually on it. Research provides you with the information on which you can base your marketing decision-making, enabling you to make informed decisions rather than stabs in the dark. It can even provide you with information that will help you avoid costly advertising and promotional mistakes.

Many local charities are very much in touch with their client group. The people who run it may even be part of that group. But as organisations grow, it is easy for them to lose touch with what the charity was originally set up to do. A charity for parents of children with birth defects may have been set up by those affected, but years later find itself run by professional staff with no direct experience of the problem. The more remote you are from the users (and funders) of your service, the more important it becomes to find out what those users and funders expect, want and need. That's where marketing research comes in. It enables you to keep close to your customers, whether those customers are service-users, funding bodies or individual donors, by providing you with information on them, their needs, thoughts, interests, motivations.

Marketing research can be used to help you find out:

■ **about your service** – what do users think about it? can they suggest any improvements? what do funders think?

■ **about your 'products'** – why do people buy them? what do they think of them? are there any gaps in your 'product line'?

■ **about your organisation** – what do people think about your name, logo and image? about your staff? about your premises?

■ **about your donors** – who are they? what types of people? where do they live? how much do they give? how can you get them to give more?

WHAT IS MARKETING RESEARCH?

You will be familiar with the term 'market research' which is, essentially, research into your market(s). 'Marketing research' is research that goes much wider. It involves market research, and also other types of research designed to help you get all the information you need to make the right marketing decisions. It might, for example, cover research into your advertising and its effectiveness.

Marketing research can take many forms – questionnaires, interviews, or reviewing existing material, for example – and can be carried out to uncover many different pieces of information. You might undertake research to find out why people give to your charity – or why they don't give. Perhaps you want to discover shortcomings in your service, or find out how you are regarded by your local community. Marketing research can provide you with the information you need. It can be used at the 'ideas stage' to gauge responses to your proposed new service, and it can be used again once the service is up and running, to establish the level of customer satisfaction. It can be used to help you develop new services and to improve existing ones.

If you look at books on marketing research, the list of contents alone will probably be enough to make you feel that it is all too complicated to undertake. It is indeed the most technical area of marketing, requiring an understanding of statistics, or at least some mathematical bent. Added to that, there's the jargon and concepts to cope with – Z scores, finite population correction and bi-variate analysis to name but three. But don't let all that put you off. You can do basic research in-house without a PhD in maths, and there are lots of friendly experts you can use if you need to commission external help.

THE BENEFITS OF RESEARCH FOR THE VOLUNTARY SECTOR

Marketing research was once the preserve of the large company; now it is common – some would say vital –

> **TRUE STORY**
>
> *After nearly 50 years of operation, one of Scotland's biggest charities, the Scottish Council for Spastics, decided to change its name. (Its sister charity in England did likewise.) The view of people with cerebral palsy, and of the charity's staff, was that the term 'spastic' had become outdated, derogatory and offensive. Research conducted among the public confirmed this view and the need for a name change. Younger parents of children with cerebral palsy said that they were put off using the charity's services because its name made it sound old-fashioned and paternalistic. A marketing advisory panel comprising external experts was established to implement the name change. Now known as Capability, it has a fresher image and is better placed to reach out to those it was set up to help. Research was an essential tool in confirming gut feeling and demonstrating the need for a new name and a modern image.*

for the public and voluntary sectors to undertake it. The benefits for non-profit organisations of carrying out research are clear. By finding out what people need from your services you can ensure that needs are met. Research can make you a more responsive, accountable and effective organisation. It can also be used to gather the necessary information to justify the existence of a threatened service, to prove the need for a new service, or to explain the demise of an existing one.

So as you can see, there are many uses for marketing research in the voluntary sector. It is not just about finding out why shoppers buy Brand X soap-powder rather than Brand Y. It can help you take a fundamental look at your products and services, your organisation as a whole, and the people who support it. Good research is the foundation stone of good marketing.

USING RESEARCH TO SHOW NEED

Many charities offer a service limited by the amount of money they have to run it. In other words, they run a resource-driven service. The money they have available sets the tone, and is a sure-fire way to the lowering of standards in the long-run. It is, of course, important for charities to live within their means, but by allowing resources to dictate the service, there is a risk that you will fail to meet the real needs of those who use your service. By contrast, a needs-led service takes need as its starting point, and then costs a service around this. If a service is to be needs-led, you must first use research to establish what the actual needs are.

Research can demonstrate need, and this in turn can be used to put pressure on statutory buyers of your service e.g. local authorities, or central funders such as government, to provide the necessary funds. It can also be used in publicity material so as to attract individual donors. Let's say that you want your local council to finance you to run a support service for male anorexics. First you need to prove the need for the service, both by establishing the scale of the problem and by showing the lack of alternative provision for this group. Such research can be used by the voluntary sector in two ways:

1. **behind the scenes** – to support an application for funding.

2. **publicly** – by publicising the research and attracting media attention, it is possible to educate and inform decision-makers and establish a favourable climate of opinion. You can make your approach for funding just at a time when funders are thinking about the problem – you come along and offer the solution.

The raw material for marketing research is information. Two types of information are available to you: secondary data (published sources of information) and primary data (newly gathered information).

SECONDARY DATA

We will consider this first because it is cheaper and generally more readily available, and therefore of more relevance to charitable organisations. Secondary data includes:

- trade journals (magazines for charities, social workers, health service professionals, housing workers etc.).

- government publications and statistics (e.g. the Census of Population, the Family Expenditure Survey, reports from the Registrar General, Monthly Digest of Statistics, Social Trends).

- research carried out by other organisations.

- information available on the Internet.

- surveys published by market research companies.

The problem with secondary data is that it is non-specific and more likely to be out of date, although it does have its uses. You can use it, for example, to establish the facts e.g. you can use the population census to find out what demographic age changes have taken place. This information can then be used to enable you to develop relevant services and to support applications for funding such services. Figures would reveal that we have an ageing population and you may respond by developing social projects for retired people, housing that is accessible to older people, or reminiscence projects for older people with memory impairment.

Large reference libraries are an obvious starting point when tracking down secondary data. Libraries these days are much more user-friendly than they used to be, and the staff will do their best to help you find the information you need. The Chartered Institute of Marketing run a library and information service, Infomark, for general marketing information. Some of the services it offers are open to non-members, although they do attract a small fee. Call Infomark on 01628 852190.

PRIMARY DATA

Primary data is not ready made. You have to gather it yourself, or commission someone else to do it for you. It is thus more expensive as well as taking longer to gather, though on the plus side it is more specific to your needs. You can get primary data by:

- **consulting experts** – academics, councillors, people affected by the issue or problem.

> **TIP**
>
> *Many professional bodies have comprehensive specialist libraries and they may allow you access if they regard your research as worthwhile. You may also be able to get access to university libraries. Ring up, explain your need and see what they say.*

> **TIP**
>
> *MORI produce reports (based on opinion gathering) covering a wide range of issues, from social attitudes and health to government policy and the environment. It is a great deal cheaper to buy one of their reports than to commission your own survey, though obviously they will be less specific to your organisation than something you commission yourself.*

- **observation** – watching reactions and behaviour e.g. showing a group of people your proposed new adverts and seeing how they react, watching to see if people look at your information bulletin board.

- **survey** – postal questionnaires, telephone surveys, personal interviews, focus groups (see below) etc.

WAYS OF GETTING THE INFORMATION YOU WANT

Aside from reviewing secondary data (also known as desk research), there are numerous ways of gathering marketing information. The best way is to ask questions. You can do this:

- in a formal way (by drawing up a questionnaire, for example).

- informally (for example by sitting down with a target group and asking them discuss various questions and issues).

- you can ask questions face-to-face (by reading them out and completing a questionnaire for the interviewee).

- by sending out a postal questionnaire.

- your questions can be direct (How much do you give to charity each year?).

- or indirect (Why do you think people are giving less money to charity now than ten years ago?).

- questions can be closed (yes/no questions, or those offering multiple choice answers).

- or open-ended (e.g. "How do you think Save Seafish could improve its image?").

> **TIP**
>
> *MORI, Gallup, Harris, NOP and the other big market research companies run regular 'omnibus' surveys which track consumer attitudes. They ask a number of very wide-ranging questions and you can pay the research company to have your own question included in one of these. It will set you back around £600. This may sound a lot, but it is a very cost-effective way of getting a national survey carried out by a leading market research organisation.*

Direct, closed questions produce very structured questionnaires which are easy to administer and analyse. On the downside, responses can be less helpful than you might wish. Take the following example:

Do you give to a charity?	❑ yes ❑ no
If yes, do you give at least once a ❑ week ❑ month ❑ year	
How much do you give in a year? ❑ less than £5 ❑ £5–£15 ❑ more than £15	

You will certainly get some interesting information, but you won't find out why they give, how they decide how often and how much to give or who they give to. Only open-ended questions can get you this sort of information. The trouble with open questions, though, is that they are difficult to record. With closed questions, your interviewer or interviewee can tick boxes on the questionnaire (though the responses you get are inevitably limited). With anything open-ended you have to do one of the following:

- tape record it (which respondents might object to. Also, the tapes will then have to be analysed, which means that someone will have to interpret them).

- get the interviewee to write responses (which is time-consuming and off-putting. It also excludes people who are illiterate or whose first language is not English).

- get the interviewer to write responses during the interview (they will need shorthand to keep up, their attention will not be as good if they are having to simultaneously write and listen, and you will be relying on their interpretation and summarising of responses, which might be unreliable).

- get the interviewer to write it up afterwards (which means relying on their memory of events and interpretation).

In spite of all the drawbacks of open-ended questions, to which we must add time and cost, they do provide better insights. It is up to you to judge which is best for you, depending on what you want to find out, how much time and money you have, who you need to interview and where they are. In practice many questionnaires contain a mix of open and closed questions.

Remember when designing questions that your starting point is your hypothesis. What are you trying to find out? What do you need to prove or disprove? Your questions must provide you with the answers you need to enable you to address your initial hypothesis.

When you ask people questions in order to obtain marketing information, you are conducting a survey. You can conduct your survey in a variety of ways (see below).

Personal Interviews

These are generally regarded as the best type of surveys, for the following reasons:

- they tend to elicit the highest level of responses.

- the interviewer can prompt respondents, or help them understand questions with which they are having difficulty.

- they can be very structured (i.e. a questionnaire with closed questions) or only slightly structured (a focus group interview – see below).

- they can take the form of a dialogue, being very much two-way and allowing respondents to ask questions as well as answer them.

There are three types of personal interviews:

1. face-to-face questionnaires.
2. one-to-one depth interviews.
3. focus group interviews.

Face-to-Face Questionnaires

This is when you read out questions from a questionnaire and record the responses given. Often these take place in the street, with passers-by being stopped and invited to help (although they can be carried out elsewhere, for example at a day centre, in a library or other public building). When stopping people in the street to ask them questions, remember that you are relying on people's goodwill to take part in your survey. Start with a brief introduction explaining why you are doing the survey and asking if they are willing to take part. It is a good idea to carry something official, such as an ID card, to reassure respondents that you are bona fide. Your opening question should be interesting and easy to answer, to give the respondent confidence. Some interviewers like to start with an open question that gets people talking. Remember that rapport is all-important in face-to-face interviews.

One-to-One Depth Interviews

A depth interview aims to uncover feelings, attitudes and motivations. It is structured (in so far as the interviewer has a framework and a clear ideas of topics/areas to be covered) but it is far less rigid than a questionnaire-based interview. Such interviews offer opportunities to delve deeper and to get qualitative insights. They can be carried out in-house using your own staff, though training will need to be provided first, as depth interviewing is an art. Ideally interviewers should be encouraging but not leading. They should be friendly and easy to talk to.

Focus Group Interviews

This is rather like a depth interview, though it involves more people – anything up to a dozen or so. The aim is for an experienced facilitator to introduce an issue and encourage the group to discuss it and offer views, opinions and insight. The interview could, for example, focus on looking at some proposed new adverts for your charity, or it could examine one of your services by bringing together a small group of service-users. When obtaining information via focus groups:

- select members of the group carefully, so they are representative of your target audience.
- used only a trained or experienced facilitator.
- structure the session so that all the necessary issues are covered.

■ if necessary, reassure participants about confidentiality.

■ ensure participants receive a copy of your findings, if appropriate, or at the very least a thank you letter and update.

Five Tips For Face-to-Face Interviews

1. If you are doing the interviews in-house, train staff and make them aware of possible errors they could introduce.

2. If interviews are being done on the street with the public, try to pick a sheltered spot such as a shopping centre, or a place where people have time to kill, such as a bus stop. (Remember, though, to select a spot that will enable you to talk to a representative group.)

3. Pay attention to how interviewers dress, and what assumptions respondents might make about them on the basis of how they look. Respondents are likely to react differently to a middle-aged woman in a Marks and Spencer suit than they are to a man in his early 20s wearing hippie-style clothing.

4. Interviewing is tiring. Give staff plenty of breaks to ensure they are refreshed and alert.

5. Ensure interviewers are properly equipped for outdoor surveys, with appropriate footwear and clothing, plenty of spare pens, a clipboard and bag or briefcase.

Mail Questionnaires

There are pros and cons to mailed questionnaires. Here are some of them:

Pros

■ questions that people might not answer truthfully face-to-face might be answered honestly in an anonymous postal questionnaire e.g. "How much do you give to charity?" or "Are you worried about getting AIDS?".

■ unlike personal interviews, which tend to have an urban bias – the woman in the High Street with a clip board comes to mind – postal questionnaires can be sent to more remote places. This is particularly useful for a national charity doing its research in-house. You couldn't possibly question people in Lands End from your HQ in John O' Groats, except by telephone (see below) and by mail.

■ respondents can work through the questionnaire at their own pace.

■ they can be cheaper than face-to-face interviews, though don't forget to take into account the cost of envelopes, printing and staff time to do the mailing, as well as the cost of the stamps.

Questionnaire return rates are increased if a stamped addressed envelope is enclosed, though this does add considerably to the cost of the exercise. (To avoid expenditure on wasted stamps, talk to Royal Mail about a Freepost address, so that you will pay the cost of postage only on those returned.)

■ you can reach many more people for the same cost as face-to-face interviews.

■ if appropriate, questionnaires can be left in your reception, where you have a captive audience with nothing better to do. (Remember to have a box available for them to post the questionnaire in and plenty of pens.)

> **TIP**
> *If you are conducting a postal survey and you plan to send tactful and encouraging reminders to those who have not completed their questionnaire, enclose a spare, as the original may have been mislaid.*

Cons

■ they usually generate a low response and thus doubt can be cast on the validity of the sample. Professional market researchers are pleased to get a response rate of 30% for postal questionnaires, though don't be surprised if you get as few as 10% back. The real issue about low response is that you need to be confident that the non-responders are not significantly different in their attitudes and opinions from those who have responded. This is not easy. Effectively you have a self-selecting sample.

■ they have to be questionnaire-based and therefore are less flexible.

■ they often comprise closed questions because respondents usually are unwilling to complete anything that will take too much time or effort.

■ you need to pay more attention to design and layout, so that the questionnaire looks attractive and easy to complete. This could mean the extra expense of having to pay a designer. Remember that attractively presented questionnaires are more likely to be completed and returned.

■ you may need to go to the trouble and expense of enclosing stamped, self-addressed envelopes to encourage returns, or setting up a 'Freepost' address.

■ you may also have to face the effort and cost of doing a follow-up mailing to encourage response.

■ unless you have an appropriate mailing list, you will need to construct one or hire one (see section on mailing lists in Chapter Ten).

■ they are not an ideal tool when surveying people with low literacy levels, or whose first language is not that used in the questionnaire.

■ because these questionnaires can be read through fully before answering, it is possible for bias to creep into the answers. 'Funnelled' questions (see below) are therefore less effective.

■ sometimes the answers you get back come from more than one person. Perhaps someone in the household starts answering the questionnaire, gets bored and finds it completed by another member.

■ the observations which interviewers can make when working face-to-face with respondents are impossible for a postal questionnaire.

It is usual, when sending out a questionnaire, to include a covering letter explaining who you are and what you do (if necessary), and what you hope to achieve through your research.

Leave a space at the end of a questionnaire for additional comments. Sometimes this can reveal some interesting and relevant insights about issues not covered in your questions.

Mailed Survey Fact File

■ there is no significant difference in response rates between questionnaires sent in a hand addressed envelope and those done with a computer-generated label.

■ self-addressed envelopes with proper postage stamps on them, when enclosed in postal questionnaires, produce a higher response than pre-printed business reply envelopes.

■ if respondents are really interested in the subject matter of your survey, they will be willing to complete even quite lengthy and detailed questionnaires.

■ the more interested respondents are in the subject matter of your questionnaire, the sooner they are likely to complete and return it.

■ the status of the person signing the covering letter has an effect on response rates: the higher the status, the higher the return figures.

■ design of postal questionnaires is important. Research has shown that response rates can be affected by typeface and type size, type of paper used and even the choice of colours used.

■ single-sided sheets produce more responses than double-sided ones

■ setting a deadline for returns increases the return rate.

TRUE STORY

An experiment was carried out whereby identical questionnaires were issued, each with a covering letter. Half the covering letters were polite and tactful, but half were short and authoritarian. Surprisingly, the questionnaires sent with the curt covering letter elicited a slightly better response!

TIP

Research has shown that sponsored surveys can elicit a better response than identical surveys that are not sponsored. For example, a survey on health workers' views about care in the community might be more successful if backing could be obtained by one or more of the professional bodies or publications representing this sector. A covering letter accompanying the survey could come from the director or chair of the professional organisation, on their own headed notepaper, thus making the mailing immediately more relevant to the recipient.

Sample Mailed Questionnaire

BRIPPINGTON ANIMAL WELFARE: HELP US TO HELP YOU TO HELP US

Thank you for helping us over the past year by making a donation to BAW. We want to make it easier for you and our other donors to support our work with sick animals, and we would welcome your input into how we can achieve this. So please spare a few minutes to complete this questionnaire.

Please circle any applicable replies. There is space for additional comments at the end of the questionnaire

1. Have many times have you given to BAW in the last year?
   ❏ once   ❏ twice   ❏ three times   ❏ more than three times (please state how many ....)

2. How have you given?
   ❏ sent a cheque   ❏ put money in collection can   ❏ both

3. Have you used one way of giving more than another during the past year?
   ❏ given mainly by cheque   ❏ mainly by can   ❏ equally by both

4. If we enabled you to give by direct debit a fixed amount monthly, direct from your bank account, would you use this facility?
   ❏ Yes   ❏ No   ❏ Would consider it

5. If yes, would you use it in place of the other ways of giving, or as an addition?
   ❏ in place of   ❏ as well as   ❏ not applicable

6. Would you consider using any of the following ways of giving to BAW?
   ❏ by credit card   ❏ by covenant   ❏ direct from your salary (for those in work)

7. Would you consider leaving money to BAW in your will?
   ❏ Yes   ❏ No   ❏ Have already made provision for a legacy to BAW

8. Would you consider organising fundraising events for BAW (such as jumble sales, raffles, sponsored events etc.)
   ❏ Yes   ❏ No

9. Any other comments? ....
   ....

Thank you for completing the questionnaire. Your comments will help us to make it easier for you to support our work. You can read about the main findings of this questionnaire in the next issue of our newsletter, which will be sent to you, and there will be an update on the action we propose to take as a result of what you have said. If you have no objection to our getting back to you to discuss your ideas, please complete your name, address and telephone number. You are, though, welcome to remain anonymous if you prefer.

OPTIONAL

Name ....

Address ....

.... Phone no. ....

We may wish to get in touch with you again about other issues and campaigns that we are involved in.

❑ Please tick here if you do not want us to contact you again.

Please return this questionnaire to:

**Felix Thompson, Brippington Animal Welfare,
Catford Street, Brippington BR1 1PR**

by July 1st

When designing your questionnaire, try to opt for questions and a format that will make it easier for you to collate the results in numerical or percentage terms. You want to be able to present your findings in a meaningful way. For example – 80% of respondents had given to BAW just once in the last year, and nearly half of these people said that a direct debit facility which took money from their bank account would encourage them to give regularly.

Telephone Surveys

Telephone surveys have benefits, though they also have a great many drawbacks, as you can see below:

Pros

■ you can reach out nationwide.

■ you can ask open ended questions.

■ research has shown that the quality of data obtained by telephone interviews is as good as that from personal interviews.

■ it can be much faster than for face-to-face interviews.

■ you can do away with the need for a paper record, which then needs to be keyed into a computer. Technology means that you can now use computer-assisted telephone interviewing (see below).

Cons

■ you might ring at an inconvenient time and alienate the respondent.

- if you are calling someone's home, they might regard this as intrusive or wonder how you got their name and number.

- there can be difficulties in building up a list of people to ring and in ensuring representative samples, though you can buy lists.

- it can run up huge phone bills, especially if you are calling long distance or during office hours.

- people might find it difficult to answer questions honestly when speaking to a real person.

- you cannot do an anonymous survey this way.

- depending on what time you call, you might find that you fail to get a representative sample e.g. calling a home number between 9am and 5pm on a weekday is not a good way of reaching working people.

- communication is limited to oral responses: surveyors cannot pick up on visual detail as they could if interviewing someone face-to-face. Visual cues which indicate that a respondent has perhaps not understood the question are lacking on the telephone.

- visual aids cannot be used. For example, this technique could not be used to test the reactions of the public to three press advertisements you were considering running.

- the growth in the number of people owning answer machines and call screening devices can pose a problem.

Computer-Assisted Telephone Interviewing (CATI)

In such surveys, respondents are telephoned and questioned in the usual way, but instead of the interviewer writing their responses, they are keyed into a computer terminal. This saves the need for later having to do this with all the results collected. It is therefore faster and cheaper, although you need to develop a computer program to deal with it, the cost of which should be added to your research budget. There are a number of companies specialising in this field who will carry out a survey for you. Computers can also be used for personal interviews (CAPI), thanks to the advent of portable laptop computers. And they can be used for self-administered testing. In this case, the questionnaire is set up on a computer screen (perhaps in your waiting room or in a shopping centre) and people can complete a questionnaire directly onto the computer. This is not widely used by charities or market research companies, but it has great potential.

> **TIP**
> Before launching a questionnaire for real, test drive it first. Check for ambiguity and clarity of questions and correct any errors. Try it out on friends and colleagues, or better still on a sample of potential respondents.

METHODOLOGY

This is jargon for how you intend to get the information you need. For example, you may decide to use a postal questionnaire plus depth interviews with a sample of donors.

DON'T LEAD THE WAY

Whichever method you use, ensure that you do not ask leading or biased questions. You must phrase all your questions carefully so that you do not inadvertently suggest that certain answers are more acceptable than others. For example, if you ask: "These days most people do not hit their children and regard it as cruel. Do you smack your children?" then you will probably not find out what really happens. Certainly you must never ask: "You don't think ... do you?" Be careful, too, of intonation when you are reading questions aloud. This can serve to lead the listener to a particular answer. For example: "Did you *agree* with the council's decision to ...?". By stressing the word 'agree', you might be influencing interviewees. You must always try to come across as neutral so as not to influence responses.

USE A FUNNEL

Many questionnaires use the 'funnel technique' to avoid bias in responses. First you ask general or unrestricted questions and gradually you start to home into more specific questions. In this way the respondent creates the frame of reference for his or her responses to the general questions. It should be a smooth process in going from the general to the specific and helps to warm up the respondent ready for more detailed questioning. For example, let's suppose you want to find out how much (or how little) people give to charity and why. Asking strangers straight out, up-front, is unlikely to provide you with the information you need: after all, the socially acceptable answer is to say that you give, and to cite a reasonable annual sum. However, this might not be true. By starting with general questions on how people divide up their weekly income, what the priorities are and what the pressures are, you are making it easier for a respondent to explain to you that as a single parent with two children and a mortgage, there is no cash left to give away. You probably would not get an answer like that without funnelling in on the issue gradually.

OPT FOR FILTERS

'Filter questions' are a useful technique. For example: "Do you use the local community centre regularly?" If a respondent answers yes, you ask them a series of questions about why they use it and what they like about it. If they answer no, you move on to the next block of questions relating to why they do not use it and what might encourage them to use it.

GETTING PERSONAL

Questions about the respondent, such as age, name, income, education, marital status and so on should be left until the end. If you start with these questions, before a rapport has been established, you will not get far. Even at the end of the interview respondents may wonder why you need to know, so it helps to preface the questions by explaining the reason and stressing confidentiality. This applies with self-completion questionnaires as well as those face-to-face and on the telephone. The only exception to this rule is when using a 'quota sample'. This is when you decide that in order to be representative, your sample must include, for example, 20% of respondents in the 18-25 age group, 25% in the 26-40 age range and so on. Here you might need to know what age respondents are at the outset, so you can meet your quota.

Sometimes you may need to ask questions that are 'difficult', threatening or on taboo subjects. For example, questions about attitudes to race, sexual orientation, religion or fears about personal health. If so, save them until the middle or near the end of the interview, so that you can build up confidence and reassurance in advance. Unless a rapport has been established, respondents will not be willing to answer these types of question. Many may be unwilling to answer them full stop. That's their right. If they terminate the interview, at least you will have gained some information from them during the first part.

WHAT'S YOUR JOB?

Sometimes you need to find out someone's occupation as part of your survey data. It appears straightforward enough, but the fact is that many people when questioned in the street will inflate their status and importance. One man claimed to be a 'transport manager' when in reality he was in charge of trolleys at a local supermarket. You may need to probe gently to find out what people actually do. Even when people are not trying to hype their job, they may give an answer that is too vague, such as "I work in housing" or "I'm a manager".

Even the order in which questions are asked can have an influence on the answers received. Survey experiments have been carried out in which half the group is asked questions in one order, and half in a different order. The responses of each group to the questions was very different, where one might have expected them to be the same.

USING QUESTIONNAIRES TO MEASURE ATTITUDES

It is easy to measure facts using questionnaires. Questions such as "How much do you give to

> **TRUE STORY**
> *Years ago, when the film 'Gone With the Wind' was current and fashionable, a survey was carried out to investigate readership of the book. When asked: "Have you read this book?", an overwhelming number of respondents said yes, as this was the socially acceptable answer. When rephrased to: "Do you intend to read 'Gone With the Wind'?" a more accurate response to the original question was elicited. Many people who perhaps did not intend to read it said that they would, but those who really had read the book made this very clear.*

charity in a year?" can be answered easily in a simple questionnaire and can be quickly collated and analysed. But what if your questions involve delving into views, such as what people think of your charity? That's where it gets harder, especially if you are using a simple, self-complete questionnaire. There are two methods that are widely used in marketing research, known as the 'Likert method of rating' and the 'semantic differential technique.' Don't let the jargon put you off! They sound horrendously complicated, but they are actually very easy and you have probably seen and possibly yourself drawn up questionnaires using these methods.

> **TIP**
>
> *Avoid too many hypothetical questions, as the information they reveal cannot always be relied upon. For example, a question like: "If charity-giving were made easier by the government, would you be likely to give more to charity?" is not likely to yield information that will be useful to you in your planning. Questions relating to people's actual experience usually elicit more accurate information.*

THE LIKERT METHOD OF RATING

Using this method, respondents are asked to state their degree of agreement or disagreement with a number of statements. For example:

'Canine Carers' is a warm and appealing name for a dog charity					
Strongly agree	Agree	Tend to agree	Tend to disagree	Disagree	Strongly disagree
❏	❏	❏	❏	❏	❏

SEMANTIC DIFFERENTIAL TECHNIQUE

Here respondents are given statements from the top and bottom of a scale and they are asked to indicate their feelings in one of seven positions offered for each set of paired statements. It sounds complicated when described like this, but the example below shows how easy it is:

The staff at our Day Centre are:	7 6 5 4 3 2 1	
friendly & courteous	❏❏❏❏❏❏❏	unfriendly & unhelpful
The food at our Day Centre is:	7 6 5 4 3 2 1	
excellent value for money	❏❏❏❏❏❏❏	poor value for money
tasty & nutritious	❏❏❏❏❏❏❏	unpalatable & unhealthy

SURVEY ERRORS

When you carry out a survey, you might expect to be able to take the results at face value and act on them. It is not always that easy. You need to be aware that errors can creep into your survey. Here are the three main ways in which this can occur:

Errors in interpreting

A respondent might misinterpret what is meant by the question, thus giving the wrong answer. For example:

Q: How much do you give to charity?

A: (scaled response from "a lot" to "none")

The first problem is that no time period is specified. Does the researcher mean over a year, a month or a week? Do they mean how much do you give in a single donation? It is not clear, and respondents are left to interpret the question, inevitably leading people to different interpretations. Also, "a lot" to one person might be "a little" to another.

Q: How many charities do you help?

> **TIP**
>
> *Sometimes your survey findings can be used to get some publicity for your charity. For example, if you carry out research to discover the level of poverty in your town, because you want to use the results in support of your application to an anti-poverty trust fund, why not also compile a news release (see Chapter Nine) and send it to your local media. You may be able to attract some media coverage for your work, helping you achieve one of the Ps in your marketing mix – promotion. Charities can even hit the national headlines. The Cats' Protection League did this recently when it carried out a survey on cat neutering, and found a newsworthy angle in the findings.*

Again interpretation is required. What is meant by 'charities'? Are local community groups or church groups included in the definition? What is meant by 'help'? Money? Time? Help in kind? Again respondents are likely to interpret this question differently, leading to inconsistent answers.

It is also possible for the interviewer to misinterpret. If the respondent is ambiguous, the interviewer might misunderstand.

Errors in reactions

Some respondents feel that in being asked to take part in a survey they are in some way regarded as special, for they have been singled out. It is possible that they will wish to present a good impression, and perhaps be tempted to give what they regard as the 'right' or socially acceptable answers. If asked whether they give to charity, or how much they give, people might be tempted to lie or exaggerate, so as not to appear mean. When asked about attitudes to controversial issues – drugs, prostitution, gay and lesbian rights, immigration etc. – you might find yourself getting the answers people think you expect, not what they really think and believe.

Interviewer-induced errors

A face-to-face interview is a social interaction. It has been discovered that in some survey interviews, the interviewee simply plays back to the interviewer the views and attitudes that they believe he/she will share. They pick up what they think are the interviewer's values and reflect these, not their own.

It is important if you are undertaking a survey that you know where errors can occur. It will enable you to avoid or take account of them.

Ten Tips For Questionnaires

1. Put questions into a logical order.

2. Avoid ambiguous wording and make your questions clear and easy to understand. One survey asked: "How did you find your last job?" expecting the reply to be "through the local paper" or "at the Job Centre". Instead many people responded "It was really interesting" or "I hated it".

3. Keep the questionnaire as short as possible: people are put off by anything too long.

4. For mailed questionnaires, make sure your address is on the questionnaire, so people know where to return it.

5. Give respondents the opportunity of returning the questionnaire anonymously if you want really truthful feedback.

6. Ensure your questions are not biased or slanted. If respondents feel you have already made up your mind about the sort of answers you want, they may not bother to complete the questionnaire.

7. Ensure that the layout of your questionnaire is clear and easy; if it looks a mess, it will put people off filling it in.

8. Make it as easy as possible to complete, by giving boxes to tick or multiple choice options to circle.

9. Limit the number of open-ended questions; they are difficult to process and off-putting to respondents.

10. Have a deadline for the return of completed questionnaires.

> **TRUE STORY**
>
> *It is really important to ensure that you use plain and simple language and short, easy-to-understand questions in surveys. What's clear to you might be gobbledygook to your respondent. Research has revealed that words in common use, such as 'incentive', 'proximity', 'discrepancy', and 'paradox' are not widely understood. It is reported that in one survey, 10% of respondents thought that 'devolution' was Jeramiah's brother! In another, one respondent, when asked for the definition of 'nostalgia', said it was Welsh for 'goodnight'. So remember to watch your language and keep it simple.*

SAMPLES

With the exception of the government's ten-yearly census, no survey can cover the whole of the population. Researchers use instead a 'sample', which is a smaller group that is representative of the 'population' they wish to survey. For example, if you wished to discover how your service was viewed by minority ethnic communities, you would need to ask them. It would be impossible to ask every minority ethnic person in the country, but you could draw up a sample that included people from across the country, with representative percentages of Bangladeshis, African Caribbeans, Chinese, Indians etc. By surveying a representative sample, rather than the entire relevant population, your survey is made more manageable and affordable.

We'll look in a moment at how to select a sample. First you need to define your population. That can take some thought. Let's look at the example above. You would need to ask:

- do we want to survey:
  - a sample of all ethnic minority people?
  - just a sample of those who have used the service?
  - just those who have never used the service?
- do we want to survey only those within the catchment area of one of our services?
- what do we mean by an ethnic minority? Does it include Irish? Travellers?
- how many people will we need to interview?

You have to be very clear on what your population is and you must ensure that your sample is representative of the population. Then you must locate your sample. Let's take the above example again. If you needed to reach Irish people in Birmingham, contacting the Irish Centre in that city would be a good starting point. Using the expertise of local councils for racial equality, and other local networks, would also be productive.

There are a number of ways of selecting a sample from your population:

Random Sampling

With random sampling, every member of your survey population has an equal chance of being selected. First you start with your 'sampling frame' – this lists everyone in the population you wish to survey, which might be:

- everyone who currently uses your service.
- all adults living in Anytown.
- subscribers to your monthly campaign newsletter.

Next you need to select a random sample from the list. You can do this in two ways:

1. **simple random sample:** give every name on the list a number and then get a computer to generate numbers randomly.

2. **systematic sample:** give every name on the list a number, select your first name randomly, then select every, say, 5th or 10th name after that.

Judgement Samples

With such samples you use your judgement as to who to interview. Such a method of sampling is useful only where you are dealing, say, with an issue requiring expert judgement. You may decide that you need only speak to a handful of key people in your local social work department, and half a dozen at a nearby NHS trust, to get the information you need on likely developments in community care provision locally.

Quota Samples

You select people in order to be sure that you have a list that represents the population. For example, you may decide that it is necessary to interview a certain percentage of men and women, a certain number of people in particular age groups or social classes.

GETTING DATA FROM OBSERVATION

We have looked at the use of questionnaires for getting marketing data. There is, though, another way; it has been used to great effect by others and is relatively easy to do – observation. Here are three real life examples of observation being used to collect important marketing information:

- **The Central Office of Information** wanted to monitor the effectiveness of its seat belt advertising campaign. Asking people if they now wore a seat-belt was likely to result in too many motorists lying and giving the socially acceptable answer. They therefore used observation: they simply counted the number of motorists wearing and not wearing their belts.

- **Honda** watched how people go about loading their car boots and used the information to redesign the Honda Civic hatchback.

- **Philips**, the shaver maker, watches men shaving (with their consent) through a two-way mirror. It uses this information to modify its products.

You may be able to think of examples in your own work where simple observation will provide you with some valuable marketing information. For example:

- using observation to see if clients look at your information board in reception; if they do, it could be an effective way of communicating with them.

- using observation to see if callers read the information (brochures, leaflets etc.) you leave in your waiting room.

There are, of course, ethical issues when it comes to covert observation, for obvious reasons.

UNDERTAKING A SURVEY

So now you know the issues and you know the jargon. The next step is to undertake the research. There are five crucial steps to this:

1. **The Research Brief:** this involves developing survey objectives. What is your hypothesis? What are you trying to prove or to find out? Who are you trying to find it out from? The brief is a broad exploration of these issues. (If you are using external consultants, you will need to give them a brief and talk through it with them. If you are doing research in-house, you still need to produce a brief. This offers colleagues who are involved an opportunity to have an input into the research.)

2. **The Research Proposal:** this is where the broad discussions held previously are now firmed up. The problem is set out, the 'population' defined, a way of selecting a sample recommended, the methodology, and estimates of time and costs worked out. If you are using consultants, they will prepare a research proposal for you to approve. If the work is being done in-house, a research proposal can be used to seek approval for the project from your committee or director, if necessary. It can also be used to ensure that everyone understands what the research is about, why it is necessary and how it is being undertaken.

3. **Data Collection:** this is the bit we most readily think of as marketing research. Here you put your methodology, recommended in your research proposal, into practice.

4. **Data Analysis and Evaluation:** having got your raw data you need to process it into a form that is meaningful. Your findings need to be analysed and related back to your original objectives.

5. **Preparing the Findings Report:** this is where you write up all the work you did in the preceding stage. You will also need to draw conclusions and make recommendations. Then you must ensure that your report does more than just sit on a shelf collecting dust. You need to ensure that you take action.

DESK DATA

Up to this point we have focused mainly on the process of gathering new information. Many organisations have existing data, in a raw form, that could be extremely useful to them if they were to analyse it. For example, if you are a national charity reliant on income from individual donors, you might find it useful to go through your records to build up a picture of where most of your donors live. You could classify people according to town or city; county; England, Scotland, Wales and Northern Ireland; north or south, east or west. There's no point in undertaking such an exercise, though, unless you have some thoughts on how you plan to use the information. You may wish to focus your publicity drive on the parts of the country where donations are low, in an attempt to boost your profile and increase donations, or to concentrate efforts on those areas where you appear to be already successful.

Desk research of this sort can help you uncover all sorts of useful information, for example:

■ your most profitable geographic areas.

■ the way people give e.g. credit card, cheque, standing order etc.

■ whether you have more male than female donors.

■ the times of the year when you receive most.

Think about what information you already have which, if properly analysed, could be helpful to you in your marketing work. Why not look at your press cuttings and see whether donations received correlate with the date and place of the appearance of positive coverage of your charity in newspapers?

USING A MARKET RESEARCH COMPANY

This is a DIY book, so the focus has been on how you can do the work. Nowadays, though, larger charities are using marketing research companies to undertake research on their behalf. If you think that commissioning a company to undertake your research will relieve you totally of the burden, you are wrong. Undoubtedly it is easier (though more expensive) to get someone else to do research for you, though there are still a number of tasks that have to be undertaken by you, namely:

■ drawing up a research brief.

■ drawing up a shortlist of companies to approach and selecting one to work with.

■ interpreting the findings (although you can pay your research company to do this for you).

■ deciding what action to take as a result of the research (you can ask your researchers to make recommendations as part of their brief).

You need to draw up a research brief so that you are clear about why you need the research, what you wish to discover, and how you will use the findings. It is also important to have a brief so that your researchers understand what exactly they are doing and to what end. A simple sample brief can be seen on the next page.

Sample Research Brief

WILLISTON FAMILY DROP-IN CENTRE

Our drop-in centre is based in the old church hall on the Williston estate, a housing estate with over 1,500 residents. It offers a range of activities free of charge for families and opens weekdays from 10am to 4pm. We were established five years ago and we are funded by the District Council.

Need for the research

At its peak two years ago the Centre attracted over 500 families every week. Now just 200 families are regularly using the Centre and numbers are gradually trailing off. The drop in usage may jeopardise our funding, leading to the closure of the Centre. We want to know why people are not using the centre, as we wish to be able to meet the needs and expectations of local people. We also wish to know from people using the Centre what they like most about it as well as what they dislike.

What we want to know

We would like to find out the following: how many people on the Williston estate and the surrounding area have heard of our drop-in centre and how; whether they have ever used it and how often; whether they still use it; if they have stopped coming, why; if they have not used it, why not and what sorts of activities we would need to offer to get them to consider attending. We also wish to know: do they know what we offer at the Centre; would they use it if it were open in the evenings? Of those who use the Centre, we want to know what they value and enjoy about it and what they would like to see changed.

What action we are considering/how we will use the research

We are considering extending our opening times and increasing the range of activities on offer. The research will provide us with the information we need to take these decisions. If activities are identified by users as being unpopular, we will consider changing, scrapping or replacing them. We intend to use parts of the research in our funding application to the council; this would relate especially to the Centre's services, which people value locally. Our application is due in by the end of September.

Sample

We wish to seek the views of teenagers and people from all age ranges through to pensioners. We want equal numbers of men and women interviewed. 80% of the sample should live on the estate and the rest in the surrounding area. Of the overall sample, we would like 25%-30% to be regular users of the Centre (i.e. visit it at least once a week). We would require our researchers to indicate how they would select the sample.

Methodology

We would like our researchers to recommend an appropriate and cost-effective methodology for this assignment.

Report

We would like a detailed report setting out all the findings. In addition we require a summary report that will set out clearly the main points in an easy to digest way. We require visual presentation on the main findings (bar charts, pie charts etc.) plus accompanying explanatory narrative. Any qualitative observations picked up during the survey may be included, in addition to the quantitative findings. We also require our researchers to make recommendations to us on future action.

Timescale

We require tenders for this assignment to be with us by midday, April 30th. We intend to have selected a market research agency by May 31st and to have the research underway by the end of June. The results of the research must be with us by July 31st.

IF IT IS A HEADACHE, TAKE AN ASPIRIN

Always discuss your brief with more than one consultancy. Each will have its own style and a distinctive approach to carrying out your brief, so aim to speak initially with three or four to give you a range of perspectives. Go by recommendation if you can. Alternatively, talk to the market researchers' trade body, the Association of Market Survey Organisations (AMSO). They can be contacted on 0171-235 1277 and will provide you with information on the types of research on offer and companies with expertise in specific sectors. There is also an organisation for those who commission marketing research, the Association of Users of Research Agencies, who can be contacted on 0171-283 7500 ext. 28323. And if all of this sounds like a headache, why not take ASPIRIN. This is an acronym that summarises the stages involved in choosing a consultancy:

A Ask around

S Source the market

P Prepare a brief

I Invite market research consultancies to present to you (at your premises or at theirs)

R Review their approach, proposals and presentations. Decide who to use

I Invite the successful consultancy to start

N Negotiate and agree the project plan and contract

When asking around, speak to other charities which they carried out research for. Try to find out what work was undertaken, whether they were any good at it, whether the work was carried out on time, whether the consultants were helpful, and whether they under-performed in any of the tasks.

When you come to interview consultants, find out the following from them:

■ do they understand what you are looking for and why?

■ how would they tackle it – are their suggestions practical and cost-effective?

■ how many consultants would be involved. You need to find out who these would be (they may not be the people presenting to you) and what their relevant experience is for the job.

■ whether trained interviewers will be used and what training they will have received.

■ what the market research consultancy's experience is of undertaking work for the non-profit sector.

- what the fee would be.

- whether this would be inclusive, and if not, what the extras would be.

- do they anticipate any problems or difficulties and if so, how do they propose to solve them?

- are they flexible – in other words, are they able to cope with a brief that may change, or a timescale that might differ to the original?

- about the consultancy – how long has it been established, who else have they worked for, what other projects or commitments will they be undertaking at the same time as your project?

- can they provide references?

You may also like to consider:

- do they come across as professional?

- do they seem to be able to think on their feet?

- did they impress us with their understanding of us as an organisation and the need for this research?

- did they appear keen to do the work?

- did they have any interesting and helpful observations to make on the brief?

Remember that your meeting with consultants should be two-way; you need to find out what they can do, and they need to find out more about you. If you aim for a meeting format that is informal but structured, you will make it easier to achieve this.

Once you have made a decision, call the successful company and commission them. Ask them to sign a contract with you which sets out your terms, expectations, deadlines, performance measures, payment details etc. Write to the unsuccessful firms to notify them.

THE EFFECTIVE MARKETING RESEARCH CHECKLIST

1. if using consultants, make sure you choose a reputable company.

2. if doing it in-house, ensure your staff are properly trained and know what they are doing.

3. check that your questions are not slanted.

4. ensure the sample is a valid one and large enough to be both relevant and credible.

5. be aware of how errors can creep in.

6. opt for the right survey method.

HAVE A GO YOURSELF

Think about what you have read on questionnaires and then take a critical look at the questionnaire below. It has been prepared by a fictitious donkey sanctuary in order to discover how the charity can improve the service it offers to members. What mistakes does it make?

TWILIGHT DONKEYS

We value your membership and wish to further improve the service we offer to members. So that we know what you think of what you get, what else you want and what you are willing to pay for it, we have produced this questionnaire. Your assistance in filling and returning it would be appreciated.

1. Do you like the monthly newsletter?
   ❑ yes ❑ no

2. Would you mind if we scrapped the newsletter or reduced it to a quarterly publication?
   ❑ yes ❑ no

3. Would you favour the introduction of an 'adopt a donkey' scheme as part of your membership? (This would give you a chance to give a donkey a name and to receive a photo and regular updates on your very own donkey.)
   ❑ yes ❑ no

4. Would you be willing to pay an extra £5 in order to adopt a donkey?
   ❑ yes ❑ no

5. Would you be more likely to renew your annual subscription if we were to give away a free poster?
   ❑ yes ❑ it would make no difference ❑ it might make a difference

6. Do you have any other comments? ....
   ....

**Return this questionnaire as soon as you can to
Twilight Donkeys.**

Discussion

There are some plus points about the questionnaire: it is brief and therefore quick to complete. It does, though, make some very important mistakes, which include:

■ Q1 is not a simple black and white issue, but it is presented as though it were. People are unlikely to like or dislike the newsletter. Some will like all of it, others will like parts only, some will like none of it, some will like some issues but not others. How can you answer with a clear cut yes or no?

- Q2 asks two questions in one, which is confusing. Scrapping the newsletter altogether is a very different option to reducing it to a quarterly.

- Q2 also raises too many 'ifs'. Some members might be happy for the newsletter to be scrapped if the membership fee were halved, for example.

- Q4 is unclear. Do they mean £5 a year? £5 per donkey? £5 a month?

- Q5 is also unclear. What would the poster be of? Donkeys? Cats? A pop group? Would there be a choice of posters? Would the poster be in colour? What size would it be? People might be influenced if the poster were a full colour A1 size donkey, but not if it were an A4 size black and white picture of Gary Glitter.

- there is no closing date for returns, which means that respondents may delay completing it and then lose it or decide not to bother. Alternatively, questionnaires may be returned in dribs and drabs, with returns coming in well after you have begun to analyse the results.

- the return address is not included. If people have to hunt around for the charity's address, they may not get around to sending it back.

CHAPTER SEVEN

IMAGE, IDENTITY AND BRANDING

What's in this chapter?

- *how to develop a positive image.*
- *how to choose the right logo and build around it a strong corporate identity.*
- *how to 'package' and promote your service or product.*
- *how to 'brand' it with its own unique identity.*
- *the importance of names and the need for name-changes.*

Like it or not, image is important. A poor image (whether justified or not) results in lower donations, you probably won't attract the best staff, and your funders might have doubts about you.

In the world of business many good products fail because they are not packaged or promoted in the right way. Don't let your packaging and promotion let you down. By 'packaging' we mean not the physical packaging (such as the wrapper on a bar of chocolate or the box a jigsaw comes in); we mean the way the product or service is presented. This might involve physical items in the form of design, logo etc. but principally it is about things like the name of a product or service, the way its benefits are presented, the words and images used to explain how it works. In short, packaging is about the many elements that go into creating an overall impression for the product. Your aim in marketing your product is to develop and package the product so that it presents the right image.

Many charitable organisations regard the concept of image development as anathema. It is simply not the done thing. It is introspective, narcissistic and irrelevant. The cause is a good one, so who needs to care about its image? If only life were so simple. The fact is that if you don't care about your image, you might find that people don't care about you. Image matters, and you can ignore yours at your peril.

Let's start by differentiating image from identity, because the two are by no means the same. Image is the way you are regarded. Identity is the visual image you shape for yourself. Let's start with image.

MULTIPLE IMAGES

No organisation has just one image. First you have a public image, which is how you are seen by your publics. In reality you might have a range of different images in this category, depending on how diverse your publics are.

- perhaps your **individual donors** see you as caring and compassionate.
- your **corporate donors** may regard you as a professional, efficient and business-like charity.
- your **staff** might regard you as a good and fair employer.

There was a time when ice cream was something children ate. Haagen-Dazs changed all that by using suggestive advertising to give their ice cream an adult, sexy appeal. A pot of Haagen-Dazs ice cream has an image a million miles away from a Mr Whippy 99 cone.

BRANDS

The first thing you need to ensure when it comes to your products is that they each have an image and an identity. This is where branding comes in. It is the way goods from one producer are distinguished from those of another, and more recently the concept of branding has been extended to services too.

A tin of Heinz baked beans looks different from a tin of Safeway own-brand baked beans. The tins are the same size and shape (and arguably the beans taste the same), but the label and design on the tins are very different. Many customers are happy to pay extra for Heinz beans because, thanks to the way the product has been packaged, branded and promoted, they feel they are getting something extra in return.

NON-TANGIBLE FACTORS

TRUE STORY

A test was carried out to establish the influence of brand names. Shoppers were asked which brand they used – consumers who said they used Brand A exclusively were given a blind test where they tried both Brand A (their supposed favourite) and Brand B. Many preferred Brand B! Some respondents were given Brand B marked as Brand A. Thinking it to be their favourite, they said that they preferred it over their actual favourite. The test shows just how powerful branding can be.

Branding involves the way a product looks and is presented, but is also about non-tangible factors. Take the example of tennis rackets. Racket A might be indistinguishable from racket B – in looks, performance, durability – and yet outsell it by 100 to one simply because of its branding. It is the same with perfume. A fragrance costing £9.99 a bottle might be outsold by another bottle of scent with a very similar chemical composition retailing at £50. Why are people prepared to pay five times as much for an almost identical product? Because of branding. In the case of the scent, the consumer is not just buying a smell, they are buying a lifestyle. They might prefer the opulent bottle and attractive carton of the expensive scent, or like the sexy and sophisticated images used in its advertising and promotion, and want to be associated with them.

Wearing the expensive fragrance makes them feel good, in a way that a £9.99 perfume from a cut-price pharmacy would not. That shows the power of branding.

BRANDING AS SHORTHAND

However, branding is not just about making your product appear in some way better. You should regard branding as a shorthand, with the name of your charity, product or service coming to represent a host of associations for your 'customers'. If you spend time and effort building a brand, people when seeing one of your products should feel confident about them. If you have confidence in the Oxfam 'brand', this confidence should extend to their shops, mail order business, campaigning wing and so on. Oxfam, having established a brand, do not have to start from scratch when launching a new product; the brand is already established and new products benefit from their relationship and association with the charity. If a new charity called Oxfamine suddenly appeared on the scene, people would regard it with suspicion. It would need to establish its credentials over a period of time before being accepted.

CREATING A BRAND

But what exactly goes into creating a brand? The ingredients are the product (or service), its packaging, name, promotion, advertising and overall presentation. A brand encompasses physical attributes (such as, with perfume, its smell), aesthetic (the design of a scent bottle), rational elements (value for money, usefulness) and emotional elements (in the case of expensive scent, it makes the wearer feel attractive or glamorous). It is this last point, the emotional one, that is very relevant for many charities. Individuals may buy your product for emotional reasons, and while other factors such as the value of your work, the probity of your organisation and so on are important factors, they do not outweigh the emotional feelings. Put together all of these factors and you have a brand – but only if your product, and its packaging and promotion, is strongly differentiated from those of competitors. Even products that are intrinsically non-brandable, such as bananas, are now branded. Labels are stuck on fruit and vegetables in supermarkets and greengrocers, and sales publicity (such as banana mobiles or posters depicting the fruit) are displayed nearby to help develop a sense of brand. People may opt for Fyffes bananas because they have confidence in that brand, even though non-branded

> **TRUE STORY**
>
> *Part of the Virgin empire's promotions strategy is to promote Richard Branson as the brand. It has paid off. A survey revealed that 34% of the population were more likely to buy a Virgin product because they like Richard Branson. Indeed 97% of people know who he is. (Few people could name other captains of industry.) Headline such as "Branson goes into trains" as opposed to "Virgin go into trains" are not uncommon. Few charities have such charismatic or popular figureheads. However, local charities can make good use of popular local personalities involved in their work. Do you have anyone who you can promote as part of your brand?*

bananas alongside taste just the same and cost considerably less. People feel they are getting more for their money.

ME TOOS

Strong or successful new brands attract 'me too' brands – imitators who hope to make capital out of copying you. If you come up with a fantastic fundraising event, it could easily be copied by other organisations, who may do a better job of exploiting its opportunities than you did. You need to be aware that good ideas will probably be copied, so do what you can to protect your ideas by promoting them in a way that closely associates them with your organisation. That way it will be difficult for others to steal them.

A strong brand will not guarantee you support, but it will tip the balance in your favour. Washing machine A might be a strong brand, but if you have to wait six weeks for delivery, you might opt for the lesser brand B instead because it offers next day delivery. And so with charities. You might be the stronger brand in the world of conservation charities, and all things being equal you would probably attract all the potential members, but if a lesser competitor offers a free newsletter, badge and poster to all new members, this might put you at a disadvantage. A strong brand is an asset, but not a guarantee. You need to develop a brand, establish its standing, and then work very hard to maintain the brand value. If other charities start offering members free gifts such as newsletters or fact sheets, you could be seen to be offering poorer value to your members. On the other hand, your USP could be that you never undertake anything gimmicky in order to attract or maintain membership. You could argue that every penny spent goes direct to the cause, with nothing wasted on car stickers, posters and the like. Such an image would be an integral part of your branding and promotion.

Brands only survive if they are kept alive by your efforts. You cannot establish a brand and then plod merrily on without any further effort. If you have established your service as innovative and pioneering, you need to keep it that way. Otherwise competitors will overtake you and your image will be worthless. If Henry Ford had stopped product development after the invention of the Model T, we would need to look not on our roads, but in the history books, to find out what business Ford was in. You too need to keep on the ball, maintain your position as the biggest, the best, the smallest, the most caring, the most efficient, or whatever it is that you are.

> **TRUE STORY**
>
> *The following companies were brand leaders in 1923: Kodak, Del Monte, Wrigley, Gillette, Coca-Cola and Goodyear. Over 70 years later they are still household names, but only because they put time, effort and money into maintaining the brand.*

BRAND EXTENSIONS

When I was a little girl Mars was synonymous with a bar of chocolate that helped you work, rest and play. Now you can buy Mars bar ice creams, mini Mars bars as bite size snacks, Mars bar Easter eggs and even Mars bar flavoured milk drinks. This is an example of an established brand extending its product lines into related new products. Because the name and the product are already known, establishing product extensions is not as difficult or expensive as if they were totally new and unfamiliar products. The brand name Mars is used as an endorsement of the quality, origin and value of the new product. The product has credibility merely because of the Mars name and associations. Charities can do this too. The Vegetarian Society was established many years ago as a charity to support vegetarians and encourage others to give up meat and fish. It now uses the Vegetarian Society name and logo as a brand, and has developed a range of new products and brand extensions which have helped it to raise its profile, campaign on vegetarian issues, raise money and attract new members. It runs vegetarian cookery courses, for example, and sells its logo to companies for use on bona fide vegetarian products (see above).

There are, of course, dangers in brand extension. The value of the brand can be diluted, and there is a risk that if one of your products suffers in some way, goes under, or attracts negative publicity, the rest of your brands could suffer. For example, if it were discovered that some products carrying the Vegetarian Society logo were not actually vegetarian (because they used animal gelatine, for example) this might damage the Vegetarian Society as a whole, leading to negative media coverage, loss of confidence and a fall-off in membership.

PRODUCT NAMES

Whether your product is the whole organisation, a particular campaign or appeal, or a service, it should have a name. That is part of its branding. Selecting the right name is vital. People take great care over naming books, children, pets, TV programmes, cars, even hurricanes. You too should spend time selecting the right name for your product or service – one that is apt, conveys the right image of the organisation, and preferably one that is concise too. The Anytown Charitable Trust for the Care and Support of Indigent Gentlewomen of Limited Means might be descriptive, but it is not very snappy and it sounds like something from the 19th century. Many charities have their roots in Victorian times, which is why their names would not look out of place in a Dickens novel. While it has been argued that a well-known charity should stick with an established name, a number of household names have successfully changed those names to keep up with the times and appeal to a new generation.

CHANGING NAME

Changing the name of your organisation is, clearly, a much bigger step than selecting a brand new name for a brand new service. It is, though, a marketing decision that you may need to consider, for your name could be working against you. Let's look at a fictitious example which illustrates the point very well – the Anytown Charitable Trust for the Care and Support of Indigent Gentlewomen of Limited Means. Let's suppose that the charity does some research to establish its donor profile, and discovers that 95% of donors are reasonably wealthy widows in their nineties. The charity hypothesises that its name and cause are the reason for its almost exclusive appeal to this group (though, of course, it could be to other factors such as where and how the charity promotes its work). What is clear is that when these supporters die, which will be sooner rather than later, the charity will probably die too. Without a fresh crop of donors, funds will soon dry up. To establish why it attracts largely from this group, it asks donors why they give their support and which other charities they support. Such research reveals that these elderly women's attitude is 'there but for the grace of God go I' and thus they offer their support out of a sense of gratitude that they are not gentlewomen of limited means. Research among a younger age group reveals that the work of the charity is regarded as essential and worthwhile once explained, but that the charity's image is a problem. They are put off helping such a fuddy-duddy sounding outfit: it comes across as remote from their experiences. The charity's name is put before the sample, along with other more zippy names such as Help Gran, Adopt a Granny and Twilight Life. It is discovered that potential donors are more likely to support a charity with a more upbeat name and image, even if it is doing the same work as the Anytown Charitable Trust for the Care and Support of Indigent Gentlewomen of Limited Means. Calling the charity Adopt a Granny means something to younger people, who can relate the name to their own grandparents and therefore to their own experience and emotions.

Your name is an important part of your image. Why do you think Norma Jean Baker changed her name to Marilyn Monroe, or Harry Webb became Cliff Richard? Names say something about a person – they can reveal gender, age, social class, ethnicity. Who is more likely to wear dreadlocks, Adrian D'Arcy-Smythe or Leeroy Garvey? Who's more likely to be a pensioner, Gladys Violet Smith or Kirsty Smith? Who's working class, Gary Richards or Jeremy Panter-Baillie? You get the picture. It is like this for charities. Which is run by a bunch of 'lefties' – Red Action Against Poverty and Injustice or The Royal Society for the Development of Assistance for the Poor and Downtrodden? Which is run by disabled activists and which by well-meaning middle class ladies – Wheelchair Rights Now and The Anytown Society for Handicapped People? Names say a lot, and we base our assumptions on them, but the reality might be very different. That's not the point, however. If potential customers are switched off by the name, and it happens in sufficient numbers, you should be concerned. People might be supporting you in spite of the name, not because of it.

The Spastics Society changed its name in 1994 to Scope. The term 'spastic' was, at the time the Spastics Society was founded, one that was applied to cerebral palsy sufferers. Now it has become a term of abuse, so a name change was inevitable. On the first anniversary of the name change, Scope had attracted nearly 40,000 new donors. It was also in talks with 25 potential corporate donors and sponsors, many of whom steered clear of the charity when it was called the Spastics Society.

Other charities, too, have successfully taken on new names. The Marriage Guidance Council was set up before co-habitation was widespread. By changing its name to Relate it stressed that it deals with relationships, whether between married couples or those living together. The National Council for Civil Liberties is now Liberty, which is much more modern sounding and has more appeal for a younger generation. If they can do it, so can you! But back to product names.

A good brand name should ideally be:

- short.
- memorable.
- meaningful, evocative or descriptive.

> **TRUE STORY**
> *To prove that names are important, how about this one. A used car salesman, aware of the dodgy reputation of his profession, described himself on his business card as a Re-owned Vehicle Re-allocation Consultant. Be aware that some name changes are downright silly!*

There are always exceptions, whether in business or the voluntary sector. Everyone has heard of Kodak, but what's it got to do with cameras? Nothing. It is a completely made-up name. Some product names had meaning originally, but while the product name is widely known, the origin of the name is not. Nylon got its name from NY for New York and LON from London: in the days before cheap transatlantic travel these were considered glamorous and alluring cities. In a similar vein, a product called Durex was launched in the 1930s. Its name came from DUrability, REliability and EXcellence. Everyone has heard of Durex and the name is now used as the generic for condoms (just as Hoover is used in place of vacuum cleaner, Biro in place of disposable pen), but how many people know how it gained its name?

Then there are the acronyms. Everyone has heard of BUPA, Britain's leading independent healthcare company, which, interestingly, is a non-profit organisation. Research shows that there is 75% spontaneous awareness among the public for the name. But how many people could say what the initials BUPA stand for? Very few would know the organisation as the British United Provident Association. So what's more important, a name that is memorable, short and snappy, even if it has no meaning or the meaning/derivation is no longer known, or a descriptive and meaningful one? There is no right answer. It is up to a charity to select a name that is the right one for them, given what they do, who they do it for, how they are funded and how they would like to be regarded. All of these factors must take into account when deciding on names.

There is something called the brand name spectrum, which you can see below:

Nucleus	➤➤	Friends of the Earth Greenpeace	➤➤	Help the Aged RSPCA Talking Newspaper Assoc.
completely free- standing, arbitrary or coined	**➤➤**	**associative or suggestive**	**➤➤**	**completely descriptive**

Arbitrary: Nucleus is a small, local charity providing support services to parents with children who have special needs. While the name does not directly relate to what the charity does, it is short, strong and memorable, and it suggests a small, close-knit and supportive group.

Associative: Friends of the Earth has associations with empathy for the planet, caring, people who are on the planet's side, who will protect it.

Descriptive: There is no doubt about what the Royal Society for the Prevention of Cruelty to Animals does.

THE CHARITY AS THE BRAND

Some companies have a clear corporate identity, and additionally they have a range of products each with their own branding. Others use their corporate brand to sell a range of other products, which may in themselves all be quite different. For example, the Sainsbury's 'own brand' is used to sell everything from champagne to toilet roll. The individual products are not given strong branding of their own; they sell by using the Sainsbury's name. Sometimes a charity finds, like Sainsbury's, that its brand is the organisation as a whole. The bits that make it up, or the services and products it provides, are not as distinctive as the organisation. For them, their own corporate identity is the brand. The branding and packaging of the whole organisation is what gives definition to the services provided by it. Its unique personality is what differentiates it from the many other charities working in the same field.

There is an Edinburgh housing association called Edinvar – the 'Edin' bit coming from 'EDIN'burgh and the 'var' from 'VAR'sity. When

> **TRUE STORY**
>
> *Electrical manufacturer Matsui sounds Japanese, but is actually British! It adopted a Japanese name because it was aware that Japanese products were considered to be reliable and 'State of the Art', and it wished the consumer to think so about its products.*

established in 1972 it housed students from the local university, but since then it has changed dramatically, with hundreds of homes, offices in other towns and nearly 100 staff. It now houses very few students and virtually no one is aware of how it came to be so named. It has worked hard to position itself as a pioneering organisation. That's its brand – Edinvar the Pioneer. It promotes all the 'firsts' it has been responsible for, and presses home its pioneering work at every opportunity, whether through newsletters, its annual report, news releases and media interviews, or through job advertising, its business plan and leaflets. So successful has it been that it is now widely regarded in its field as an innovative and forward-thinking organisation. The interest taken in it is far beyond its size, and its reputation has now spread to Europe. This has stood it in good stead in attracting funding, doing deals and forging partnerships with the big league, and attracting and keeping the best staff. By ensuring that its innovative work is geared towards providing the best possible service to its users, it protects its brand name. New services launched by Edinvar, such as its community care service, benefit from their association with the Edinvar brand.

BRANDING SERVICES

Traditionally branding has been associated with products; increasingly the service sector is taking an interest in branding its services so they have a perceived unique and differentiated personality. Personality is promoted via the company's people and the key elements of the provision of its service, such as efficiency, cost-effectiveness, speed, courtesy etc. For service providers it is important to develop a perception in the market place of your individual personality which sets you apart from the competition. Take British Airways, which describes itself as the world's favourite airline. That's quite a claim! How can an airline differentiate itself from the others when the chances are that it flies to the same places as the rest, has the same flight times, the same fares, flies from the same airports and so on? The world's favourite airline slogan is one that it uses to help set it apart. It also does it through its packaging. There is a unity of design from bag tags and tickets through to staff uniforms and the upholstery and colours within the plane. It would be foolish for charities to spend on designer uniforms or expensive interior-designed offices, but there is still a lesson there for the voluntary sector. Visual identity, combined with good quality of service, can be the hallmarks that help you to differentiate what you provide from what is available elsewhere.

REPOSITIONING THE BRAND

You might find yourself with a brand image that you do not want any longer. Many third world charities used to promote themselves as aid agencies; they raised money for third world aid and to relieve the symptoms of poverty and disaster. There came a time, however, when this was regarded as a paternalistic, even a racist approach.

Progressive third world charities decided to reposition and repackage themselves. Instead of using images of emaciated children with begging bowls and swollen bellies, they started using positive imagery. Instead of showing third world people as helpless victims they were presented as people who, with assistance in the form of money or expertise, could take control of their own destiny. Instead of appealing to people using pity, they appealed using economic arguments. Instead of fighting the symptoms they began to address the causes. Such charities saw their donor profile change. Instead of attracting older, more affluent people to whom their previous approaches had appealed, they now attracted younger people with an interest in the political and economic system that maintains underdevelopment and an understanding of the colonial process that had caused it. In such cases the charities decided that there was a need to refocus their work; the changed donor profile was a side effect of that, not an aim. Indeed many charities found that their new supporters had less money to give, and that in fact the emotional line they had previously taken had served them well in terms of attracting money.

Some commercial companies have repositioned their brand too, specifically in order to attract new and different customers. Lucozade is the text book example that is always cited as the classic repositioning exercise. Developed in the 1920s, Lucozade was a glucose drink for invalids and convalescents, particularly sick children. How many of us cannot remember being given a large bottle wrapped in mustard-coloured cellophane? In 1983 the drink was dramatically repositioned using the British Olympic decathlon gold medallist Daley Thompson. He promoted Lucozade as a dynamic, vital sports drink. The big bottles and the cellophane disappeared, and cans and one-drink mini bottles were introduced, along with Lucozade glucose tablets and isotonic sports Lucozade. Although the composition of the drink has not changed, its radical repositioning has resulted in today's youngsters regarding it as a healthy sports drink, not something for sick children. Now, instead of drinking Lucozade on the one or two occasions a year that they are ill, children (and adults) are drinking it perhaps once or twice a day! Clearly that kind of repositioning has a positive effect on sales of the product.

What are the lessons here for charities? First, you can take your existing product and turn it into something that appeals to a very different audience. The way you package and promote it can achieve this for you, and if you are a charity that uses celebrities, your choice will be a crucial factor in positioning you where you want to be. Second, you can take elements of what you offer, but alter them in a minor way so as to appeal to your new audience. Lucozade produced cans in place of large bottles, thus making the drink more practical for sports people. You might find that an alteration to your existing product would make it more attractive to or appropriate for your new audience. If you aim to attract students as members, they might find it easier to pay their subscription monthly by direct debit rather than annually via a credit card, for example.

VISUAL IMAGE

Like it or not, visual image is important and consideration needs to be given to it as part of your marketing activities. Just as people are often judged by how they look, your organisations will be judged on its letterhead, annual report, office and staff. The way things look counts. The most obvious aspect of your visual identity will be your logo; other elements will stem from this. If you don't have a logo, or you are considering a new one, here's what you need to do:

Logo Low-Down

1. decide what you want your logo to say about you, what sort of image it should portray (e.g. caring, efficient, welcoming, concerned with children, concerned with trees and the environment).

2. write down your ideas for how this could be achieved. Sketch your ideas if you find it easier.

3. write down any words or straplines (a brief statement or description of your work) that need to be incorporated into the design.

4. decide whether your logo will be a design in its own right, or just a stylised version of your name (your designer can advise you on this).

5. decide how many colours your logo will be (the more colours you use, the higher the printing costs will be for your stationery and other materials – two-colour logos are quite acceptable).

6. brief your chosen designer about your work and your ideas for a logo. Consider asking the designer to design a logo that will also reproduce well in one colour and that will photocopy and fax clearly.

7. look over the various options prepared for you by your designer, and if necessary commission further drawings. Make sure you see the logo on letterheads, compliments slips etc. to get a proper feel for how it will look in use.

8. select a design and get the final artwork produced.

The colours you select for your logo are known as your 'corporate colours'. You should use them whenever possible to reinforce your visual identity. For example, if your colours are yellow and your staff wear sweatshirts as uniforms, get them to wear yellow sweatshirts. Use pale yellow paper for memos on your noticeboard, perhaps display yellow flowers in your reception. Gimmicky? No. It helps make you more memorable, which is vital to effective promotion.

CHAPTER EIGHT

PROMOTION – ADVERTISING

What's in this chapter?

■ *how to select the right medium – pros and cons of different advertising media.*

■ *how to set your advertising objectives.*

■ *producing adverts that work.*

■ *advertorials/advertising features.*

■ *choosing and using an ad agency.*

■ *legal requirements of advertising.*

■ *avoiding adverts that exploit or patronise.*

■ *factors affecting the cost of advertising.*

■ *monitoring and evaluating your advertising.*

Marketing and promotion are often thought of as identical, but in reality the latter is an aspect of the former. It is, however, a very important aspect, one that deserves four whole chapters devoted to it. In this chapter you can see how media advertising can be used as a promotional tool.

P FOR PROMOTION

Promotion is one of the four Ps of the 'marketing mix' (see Chapter Thirteen). Some companies focus their energies and budget on this one P, for obvious reasons. What's the point in having a terrific product, which is in the right place at the right price if no one knows about it? Promotion is important if you want people to know about your services and products, whether they are users or donors. You need to tell homeless people that you run a free hostel. Otherwise they will not know about it and will not use it. You need to tell donors about how well used your hostel is and how there is a pressing need for another one to help keep up with demand. Otherwise they won't send in a donation.

Charities have a host of promotional vehicles to select from. Some are easier than others to use, some are more expensive, some have a bigger impact. Those you opt for depend on your budget, the time available to you, and what you intend to promote. Why opt for TV advertising (even if you could afford it) when a cheap leaflet would produce the same result?

Your promotional tools are:

- advertising – TV, radio and press.
- direct mail advertising.
- editorial coverage via public relations.
- promotional leaflets.
- newsletters.
- other publications, including annual reports, brochures and posters.
- exhibitions.
- open days.
- roadshows.
- talks and seminars.

Charities and voluntary organisations can advertise in many places and in many different ways. Everything from eggshells to bus shelters is possible, but we will concentrate in this chapter on media advertising (i.e. TV, radio, newspapers and magazines). Chapter Nine will examine public relations as a promotional tool. Chapter Ten will look at direct mail advertising and Chapter Eleven will explore other ways of promoting a message.

Advertising has a glamorous image and the people who work in it are sometimes regarded with envy. But of course, there's advertising and there's advertising. You don't have to opt for an expensive advertising agency in the Saatchi and Saatchi league; a display advert penned in-house for your local paper might suffice – and does for many charities. So whether your budget is big and national press advertising an option, or whether it is small and you'll be doing everything in-house, there might be space in your promotional strategy for some advertising.

Charity advertising has become both sophisticated and widespread. Open up The Guardian, The Times, a Sunday newspaper, a tabloid, a trade publication and chances are that you will see charity advertising. Look at a bill board in the street and you may well see something there too. Local and national commercial radio also carries a fair amount of charity advertising. Even TV does some, although cost is the main reason why many charities are kept off our screens. Some advertising is placed to publicise an issue – such as animal cruelty, child abuse, environmental matters. Some seeks money – for aid and other worthy causes. Some just promotes the work of a charity and publicises the name.

As this book is a DIY guide, we will look here mainly at press advertising, which you can often do in-house; if you are planning TV or radio advertising, you will probably need to use an external advertising agency (see page 109 for details of how to select an advertising agency).

Ten Uses For Media Advertising

You can use media advertising to:

1. attract staff.

2. encourage volunteers.

3. ask for donations (of goods and money).

4. get people to consider leaving you a legacy or other gift.

5. promote membership of your organisation.

6. promote your name and your work, or remind people that you are still there.

7. promote an issue or cause – to inform, educate or campaign.

8. advertise an event.

9. advertise a service.

10. sell a product.

If you are considering media advertising, the first question is what sort of advertising you should opt for.

WHICH MEDIUM?

Budget is often a primary factor when it comes to selecting the best advertising medium. Apart from the obvious considerations such as what you can afford, you also need to consider what is appropriate, what will achieve your objectives most cost-effectively (see below) and what will reach your target. An advert in Playboy might prove effective in terms of attracting donations, but is it appropriate? A TV advert might lead donors to question how you can afford it. A national newspaper advert for a local event would be madness. Targeting is a fundamental advertising issue. So when considering advertising as a promotional tool, start by asking:

■ what do we want to advertise and why? What are our **objectives**? (see below).

■ who do we want to reach? What is our **target audience**? (decision-makers? wealthy people likely to leave legacies? 'trendy lefties' likely to support our cause? animal lovers? people interested in politics? anyone living in Greater Manchester?).

■ what do we want to say to them? What are our **key messages**?

■ how can we achieve this? What advertising **channels** are open to us that will allow us to promote these messages to these audiences?

- **how often** would we need to advertise to get our message across successfully and **how big**/long would our advert need to be?

- what is our **budget**? What is the cost of the various options? Which can we afford?

- what are the **hidden costs**? e.g. placing an advert in the national press involves the cost of buying the space, but you also need to consider the cost of commissioning an advertising agency to design the advert, which will include the cost of photography, copywriting, artwork etc. It is the same with radio adverts. The advert needs to be scripted, actors/voice-over artists commissioned, singers/musicians taken on if necessary etc. That's all on top of the cost of buying the airtime.

- could we use this money more effectively in **another way**?

- **who else** advertises here? Is there any clash or conflict? Could we end up in competition with a more 'attractive' or appealing charity?

- what would **our supporters** think? Might they feel that we were wasting their money on advertising when it should go straight to the user?

When it comes to media advertising, you have various options open to you:

- local and regional paid-for press.
- local freebies.
- national press.
- trade, consumer and specialist publications.
- local commercial radio.
- national commercial radio.
- commercial TV.

Let's look at each in turn:

Local Paid-For Newspapers

Pros:

- local newspapers are an excellent way of geographical targeting. Some cover just a town or city, while others – such as the Yorkshire Post or The Scotsman – cover a whole region.

- the newspaper will sometimes help you to design the advert for free, although don't expect more than some basic layout of your text and logo.

- a representative from the newspaper will be happy to come and see you and discuss options and ideas with you.

- as there is no long lead-in time, you can place an advert at very short notice.

- you can make use of coupon responses, essential if you want people to write in for information or send in a donation. (If you are using a coupon as part of your advert, it is easy to code it so that you can tell which publication it appeared in, and even on which day. This is invaluable when it comes to discovering which adverts were most effective.)

- it can be quite cheap, especially if you are using classified adverts.

- your advert can be read and re-read.

Cons:

- your advert has to compete for attention.

- people buy newspapers primarily for the news, not the adverts, so many just scan ads without reading them.

- reproduction can be poor, though it is getting better.

- daily and even weekly newspapers have a very short shelf-life, which reduces the chances of your advert being seen.

- there is wastage: you should never assume that just because the official readership is 100,000 people, all of them will read your advert. With radio and TV advertising, the advert is played to the viewer or listener. With press advertising the reader must make the effort to read your advert.

- press adverts are static and two-dimensional.

Local Freesheets

Pros:

- they are cheap to advertise in and, because they are free and hand-delivered, they reach most households.

- many people look forward to their local freebie, and do read both the news and the adverts.

- some free newspapers cover a very small area, allowing very precise geographical targeting.

- coupon responses can be used.

- it can be very cheap, especially if you are using classified adverts.

- your advert can be re-read.

Cons:

■ their only revenue is advertising, so freebies carry many more adverts than a paid-for newspaper. This means that your advert will have to compete for attention with many more adverts.

■ a significant number of people make a point of never reading their freesheet, binning it on receipt. When someone takes the trouble to buy a paper, they will find the time to read it. Something delivered free to their door may not be valued in the same way.

■ many freesheets are so locally-based that they do not reach a good cross-section of the population.

■ free papers are not always regarded as 'real' newspapers.

■ not all readers will read your advert.

National Newspapers

Pros:

■ national broadsheet papers are read by decision-makers and professionals, so it is a good way of reaching these audiences.

■ each paper has a very clear readership profile, so targeting is easy.

■ there are fewer adverts to compete with than in local papers.

■ you can place an advert at short notice.

■ they are ideal for national organisations to reach a wide audience.

■ coupon responses can be used.

■ although more expensive than local papers, national press advertising can be affordable if you use their classified sections.

■ your advert can be read and re-read.

Cons:

■ although some national papers have a geographical bias (e.g. more readers in the north of England than in the south), geographical targeting is clearly much poorer than for local papers, so they are generally of less use to local or regional charities. Some papers produce regional issues (e.g. the Daily Mail) or have a Scottish edition, so this does help targeting.

■ it is much more expensive than advertising in local papers.

■ reproduction can be poor.

■ daily newspapers have an even shorter shelf-life than weekly freesheets, though the Sunday papers do lie around for longer.

■ unlike a local or free paper, national papers often have a more stylish format and the adverts that appear in them are more likely to be properly designed (unless they are display adverts). This will add to your costs, for you will have to buy-in design in addition to buying the space. Many papers will want 'camera ready artwork', which you will need a designer to prepare for you.

■ not all readers will read your advert.

Professional/Trade Magazines

Pros:

■ audience targeting is much easier – nurses read Nursing Standard and architects read Architects' Journal, so you can easily reach a particular profession or interest group.

■ there is generally better reproduction and fewer adverts to compete with (except in the trade publications that are given away free).

■ the shelf-life is a great deal longer than for newspapers (particularly for monthly publications)

■ most trade publications are passed around the office and therefore read by more than one person.

■ they are often filed for reference, too, thus making them even more long-lasting.

■ coupon responses can be used.

Cons:

■ you may have to advertise in a number of journals to reach all of your audiences, whereas a newspaper advert in the right paper would allow you to reach them in one go.

■ the longer lead-in times mean that you have to plan ahead.

■ you may be asked to provide 'camera ready artwork' and this will involve engaging a graphic designer.

Local Commercial Radio

Pros:

■ with local radio it is possible to target geographically.

■ it tends not to attract social classes A and B, so if you want to target C1s, Ds and Es, it is ideal.

■ it can work out cheaper than you might imagine, and most stations have a member of staff available to help and advise.

■ many local stations have a very loyal following.

- most homes have more than one radio and 95% of all cars have one, so there are many opportunities for people to tune in, whether at home or in the car.

- unlike press advertising, dimension and life is added to radio adverts with the use of voice, music and sound effects.

Cons:

- local radio is frequently on as background noise, with listeners doing other things while half-listening.

- it is more transient than a newspaper advert, which can sit around for days and weeks, and can be looked at again and again.

- unlike a coupon response in a newspaper or magazine advert, it is more difficult to respond to radio adverts. Often you need to have a pen and paper handy to take down the details, so it requires more effort from the listener for you to get a response.

- you will need to budget for making the advert, as well as buying the airtime. This will involve a copywriter, a voice-over artist and perhaps costs for music too.

- unlike both TV and press advertising, radio is not visual.

> **TIP**
>
> *The medium is as important as the message. A brilliant advert placed in the wrong newspaper will be a waste of money. Take the same care when deciding where to advertise as you do when deciding what to advertise.*

National Commercial Radio

Pros:

- the growth in specialist channels in national commercial radio, such as Classic FM, enable certain social groups to be targeted. In the case of Classic FM, social classes A, B and C1 can easily be reached.

- it offers opportunities to reach a large number of people for a great deal less than TV advertising.

Cons:

- apart from talk radio, such as BBC Radio 4 (which is, in any case, not commercial and therefore does not carry advertising) radio is often not actively listened to.

- all the drawbacks of local radio also apply to national advertising.

Commercial TV

Pros:

- film is a powerful and persuasive medium, and a clever advert can change people's hearts and minds.

- you can reach a wide audience.

- you can target geographically (by advertising on one or more of the local networks) or buy airtime on all of them to ensure national coverage.

- you can decide what time you want your advert to appear and during which programme, so as to reach the right audience.

- you can enter people's homes.

- little effort is required by the viewer, as your advert is presented to them.

Cons:

- TV is very much at the glamorous end of advertising. It is expensive, both to buy airtime and to make the advert for screening. It is highly unlikely that you could do the job yourself; you would require either a skilled in-house communications team and/or an advertising consultancy. A few charities have advertised on TV, but for most it is both unaffordable and inappropriate.

- with the advent of video recorders, many people are taping programmes and then fast-forwarding during the adverts, and this has become a real concern to the advertising industry.

- many viewers 'channel hop' using their remote control during commercial breaks.

- it is difficult to get across a complicated message in a few seconds.

- TV advertising is transient; it is over in a flash and cannot be retained in the way that a press advert can.

SETTING OBJECTIVES

Never place an advert just because it seemed like a good idea at the time, or because there was a special offer with reduced rates. You need to be absolutely clear about your objectives before you advertise. Your objectives need to be specific and measurable. It is no good saying "we want to advertise in order to raise awareness." That's too general and unfocused an objective. The following objectives are measurable:

We want to advertise in order to:

- attract 600 new members or

- attract total donations of £500,000 or

- attract 100 enquiries about our service, leading to 50 people being offered help or

■ generate an increase of 50% in the number of calls received by our helpline

You also need to put in some kind of timescale, for example:

■ we wish to attract 600 new members within one month of our advert appearing.

■ we want to attract donations of £500,000 within six months of our advertising campaign ending, all of them as a direct result of the campaign.

It is obvious why you need to set objectives. By being clear what you want to achieve from your advertising campaign, you can measure in an objective way whether you have been successful. Objective-setting will also help you to select the right advertising medium to achieve the results you are looking for.

TRUE STORY

A newspaper decided to send marketing managers some sharply tipped metal arrows, as a gimmicky demonstration of its proficiency at targeting readers. It was an effective gimmick, but the newspaper landed up in trouble with the Advertising Standards Authority, who said that the mailing of a potentially offensive weapon was not a suitable promotional item.

ADVERTS IN ISOLATION

Too many organisations, charitable and commercial, place an advert as a knee-jerk response. They see their membership falling or donations sliding, for example, and regard a hastily-placed advert as the solution. If this is your attitude, advertising will fail you. You need to see advertising as one part of your marketing strategy. It should be built into the strategy, and carefully planned alongside your other marketing activity.

ADVERTS THAT WORK

Once you have decided on a budget and come up with the advertising medium that you can afford, and one that will reach the necessary audience, you need to work on the advert itself. Producing effective advertising copy is an art. It has been suggested that we see between 1,000 and 1,500 sales messages every day, on TV, buses, posters and so on. Of these we remember just seven to ten. In other words, the vast majority of advertising just passes us by. You need to ensure that money you spend on advertising produces adverts that fall into the memorable category. You can do this by using the services of an advertising agency (we will look later at choosing and using an agency), or doing it well in-house.

But before you even put pen to paper you need to do your homework. You must:

■ **understand your audience** – you need to know who you are writing for, if you are to stand a chance of communicating with them effectively.

■ **know the competition** – unless you know what they are offering, how can you offer something different or better?

■ **know your UBP** – your Unique Buying Point. This is different from a USP (Unique Selling Point) because it takes as its starting point what is of interest and importance to the buyer. USPs are product-centred. UBPs focus on what counts for the buyer, at whom your advert is aimed.

Once you are clear on the above you are ready to start on your advert.

DIY ADVERTISING COPY

This section will explain how to produce copy for the print media. Writing scripts for radio and TV is very specialised and it is probably better to use an advertising company to help you with your commercial.

> **TRUE STORY**
> *During the Second World War, Stork margarine was heavily advertised, even though it could not be bought on ration coupons. When the war ended and Stork became available again, the company ran an advert showing a stork in prisoners' uniform being released from prison. Many products were forgotten about during the six year war, but Stork had no difficulty in making its comeback.*

There is no doubt that a good professional will produce a better advert than a keen, if talented, amateur. Nevertheless, it is possible to produce effective press advertising in-house, as long as you know what you are doing, what works and what doesn't, and so long as you can get someone to share with you the tricks of the trade. Here are some useful tips. First of all remember that good advertising should employ the AIDA formula:

> **TIP**
> *When you see the artwork for your advertisement (whether produced in-house or by an agency) ask to see it presented as it would actually appear. In other words, take a page from the newspaper in which it will be placed, and substitute your own advert for an existing one. Now photocopy it so it looks more like newsprint. An advert on its own has more impact than when seen surrounded by the text of a newspaper.*

■ it should attract **Attention** so that people see it and read it. Strong photographs or other imagery can help, as can an arresting headline, bold colours (or striking use of black and white in a colour publication), good design, or a combination of these to achieve something attention-grabbing. Remember that your advert will be competing with many others, so it must stand out and attract attention.

■ it must develop in the reader an **Interest** in your product or service.

■ it should create **Desire** – to use your service, or buy your products, or take out membership, or work with you or for you, or donate to you, or campaign for your cause, or support you in some other way. Study commercial adverts and see what techniques they employ to stimulate desire; if people are willing to pay over the odds for a pair a jeans or a new perfume, it shows the power of advertising.

■ it must prompt **Action** – there's no point in producing an advert that is arresting, encourages interest in your service and a desire to use it, if nothing happens thereafter. Your advert should be designed so as to persuade donors to give and to make it easy for them to take action (perhaps with a tear-off slip) or to get people to ring up your free advice line (by publicising the number and opening times).

Some advertisers attract attention to their adverts by being deliberately different and unexpected. Take this example. What do you think it is advertising?

> *"Guinea Bissau is one of the poorest countries in the world and is arguably the most underdeveloped country in Africa. Economic aid was cut in 1989 and the region has been struggling to maintain its infrastructure ever since. The European Development Fund has been helping by introducing a more efficient farming policy, and has created a 50,000 hectare project devoted to maize, cotton and rice..."*

The advert continues in this vein for several paragraphs more. Is it an advert for Oxfam? No. Voluntary Service Overseas? No. It is a car advert! I don't normally read car adverts but I read this one. Why? Because it was so totally unexpected that I kept reading in order to find out what the economy of Guinea Bissau had to do with the up-market and expensive Land Rover. Six paragraphs later I found out. It is good on hazardous terrains and in monsoons that turn roads to rivers of mud, as happens in Guinea Bissau. I wasn't persuaded to buy a Land Rover, but I did read the sort of advert that I would normally ignore.

HOW DO WE 'READ' ADVERTS?

A great deal of research has been carried out to discover how people 'read' an advert. There is a definite route which people's eyes take when they see an advert for the first time.

Our Eye Path

1. First of all they go to the picture, so it goes without saying that the one you opt for in your adverts should be large, dramatic and attention-grabbing.

2. Next their eye moves to the headline. Again you must ensure that yours is snappy and hard hitting. Only one in five readers make it beyond the headline.

3. Readers then move on to the bottom right-hand corner of the page, which is where most advertisers place their name and logo. The majority of readers will get no further than this.

4. For those that do, the caption on the photo is the bit they read next.

5. This is followed by a scan of the cross heading, other illustrations and graphs, sub-headings and so on.

6. only after all this do people begin on the 'body text' – the main part of your advert.

The lesson in all this is simple. Don't rely on your text to get people interested; most won't ever get this far. If your picture and headline are not arresting enough to attract readers into your advert, you are on to a loser.

THE PICTURE PLUS HEADLINE FORMULA

A tried and tested formula, which is used by the world's biggest companies, and their advertising agencies, is the dramatic-picture-plus-intriguing (or witty)-headline. It works. An advert for Honda, produced to show how economical the Honda Civic is when it comes to fuel consumption, showed a car alongside a petrol pump, with the headline: "Avoid painful fillings." Charities can, and do, use this formula too. Take this advert for the Guide Dogs for the Blind Association. A photo of a man's face with dogs' eyes reads: "No surgeon in the world can help this blind man see. But a dog can."

It works because it tells a story in a picture and a few words, the image is powerful, the headline clever. That's what you should aim for. Here's another charity example. The headline reads: "Like this coat? The last owner was shot in it." A photograph of a leopard skin coat illustrates the headline.

A picture and headline should work together, with each telling its half of the story. A picture that simply repeats the headline, or vice versa, will not produce the desired effect. Each needs the other to make sense, and together they should produce a strong enough message to stand alone, without any body text. Obviously you should have body text, to give the detail, but you should aim for something that can work well without it.

HEADLINES THAT WORK

Your headline is one of the key elements of your advert. 80% of readers will get no further than it, so you need to work hard to ensure that it does its

> **TRUE STORY**
>
> *Greenpeace produced a cinema advert directed by Roger Corman, who has made over 300 movies and was responsible for talent-spotting the likes of Martin Scorsese, Francis Coppola, Robert De Niro and Jack Nicholson. The advert includes both violence and nudity, in the form of a naked Mother Earth (symbolising the planet) gradually and innocently being destroyed by doe-eyed children. These shock tactics were designed to attract the attention of cinema-goers. On the back of its advertising, Greenpeace also attracted a great deal of editorial comment, much of it negative.*

> **TRUE STORY**
>
> *In 1995 the charity Children First ran an advert with a photo of a child's frightened face, with the headline "If you only give money to animals: she's been treated like one all her life." As a result of the advert a number of animal charities wrote in objecting to the implication in the advert, as they saw it, that people who care about animals do not care about children. Other correspondence putting forward different views followed, turning an advertising campaign into something much more high profile that was carried into the letters pages.*

> **TIP**
>
> *In newspaper adverts, 'reversed out' copy (where text is not printed, but the surrounding paper is, making the text appear to be printed the same colour as the paper) is less likely to be read than ordinary text. Therefore, try to avoid it.*

job well. If you neglect your headline, you are wasting 80% of your advertising budget. You can make your headline more effective by:

1. using **why** in the headline. "Why ten million Britons have supported X Charity" is better than "Ten million Britons have supported..." The first makes people wonder, the second leaves them thinking "so what?"

2. using **how**. For example, an advert encouraging donors to give by covenant, thus enabling the charity to reclaim the tax, might read "How to give us 40p in the pound extra – at no cost to you"

3. using **do**. An effective ACTIONAID advert read: "Do you really need 50p more than she does?" and was accompanied by an appealing photograph of a child in Southern India.

4. using a **signpost** to alert your intended audience. For example, a fundraising advert for a children's hospice could be headlined: "PARENTS – How would you feel if your child was dying?" An advert for breast cancer screening might read: "WOMEN OVER 50 – breast cancer is a real killer in your age group, but free screening ..."

TRUE STORY

One anti-fur campaign produced an advert that met all the criteria for a successful advert. It showed an eye-catching photo of an attractive woman in high heels and a fur coat, headlined: "It takes 20 dumb animals to make this coat but only one dumb animal to wear it." The advert was instantly branded sexist and many potential supporters were put off the charity for ever, even though they supported the cause. Clearly you have to be careful in your advertising not to alienate potential supporters.

TIP

Full colour advertisements in magazines attract twice the readership of black and white ones, so consider this when making a decision about which to use. And remember that provided the quality of the reproduction is good, photographs have greater credibility than artwork and generate about 25% more recall.

The first two headlines above, and the final one, could work without an illustration, and are therefore ideal for charities who have a really tight budget and must produce all adverts in-house. Simply by using a strong headline and attractive typesetting, you can produce an advert in-house that costs very little to develop. Another headline that works well without a photo is this one for the blood transfusion service: "What if they only gave blood to people who were donors?" This is strong enough to stand without any body copy at all, and would make a good advert for the side of a bus, for example. A charity raising £11 million for a hospital known locally as the Sick Kids used bus advertising which centred around headlines alone. One memorable ad read: "This bus passes by the Sick Kids. Make sure you don't." It was clever because of the pun and because of the fact that it was displayed on buses passing the hospital, thus serving as a further reminder to passengers.

THE BODY TEXT

Remember that only 20% of those looking at your advert will get this far. However, those who make it are likely to be interested in what you have to say. Your body text needs to explain your headline (and photo, if you used one). It is your chance to give more detail, to offer any facts and information, and generally to draw the reader in. But be careful.

- ✗ **don't** waffle.

- ✗ **don't** say too much; your reader will have trouble taking it all in.

- ✗ **don't** present too many ideas or propositions; it will confuse.

- ✗ **don't** use too much unbroken text or small print; it will cause a headache.

- ✔ **do** use short sentences and short paragraphs.

- ✔ **do** use questions as subheads, to keep readers' interest. For example: "Would you like to make the world a better place for your children?".

- ✔ **do** use the first person – lots of 'we', 'you', 'your' etc.

ADVERTS FOR DONORS

Much charity advertising is aimed at attracting donations. If you have found that your attempts at advertising have cost as much as the money you have attracted, you are clearly doing something wrong. You may have chosen the wrong publication or the wrong time of year, or perhaps you got the copy wrong. There are various ways of achieving better results from adverts seeking money:

Eight Ways to Improve Your Chances

1. Never just ask for cash. Always try to explain how a small amount of cash can make a difference. For example, instead of simply asking for money to combat blindness in the Third World, why not say "Your £5 can make Asuk see his grandson for the first time." Don't ask for money to help the environment, say "£10 will plant a tree for future generations". This way people feel that even though they are giving perhaps just a small amount, it really will help.

2. When asking for money, provide a menu of options. List various items, with a price tag alongside, enabling donors to opt for an amount e.g. £1 could pay for a dozen wild flowers, £10 would pay for a tree, £200 could help plant a new forest.

3. If you are suggesting amounts of money to give, it is best to list the options in ascending order, so that the donor feels more generous the higher up the list they go. Listing in descending order makes donors feel mean if they go too low, and may well put them off giving at all.

4. If you can, try to bring your advert to life by using real people. The example above, "Your £5 can make Asuk see his grandson

for the first time," is so much more powerful than a headline about the problem and effects of Third World blindness. People can relate to other people, and put themselves in their shoes. It is much harder to be moved by abstract concepts or global problems.

5. Always include an option to give a very small amount of money. To some people £15 is a huge sum, yet many charities start their options with this as the minimum. It may encourage some people to give a little more than they otherwise would, but it can also put a great many off giving anything at all.

6. Keep your copy brief and your request simple. Complex advertisements fail because many readers do not have the time or energy to tackle a complicated advert with too many messages and too much detail.

7. Caption your illustrations: they attract twice the readership of the main text.

8. Include a line space between paragraphs: this increases readership by 12%.

MAKING ACTION EASY

Remember the AIDA formula? The last A stands for action, and your task is to design an advert that makes clear what action is required, and enables respondents to take it with ease. There are various ways you can do this.

1. **Use a coupon response**. This makes it really easy for readers to send in for further information or to mail you a donation. If you are using this device, remember to put your address on the coupon rather than in the body of the advertisement; if a reader loses the advert having cut off the coupon, they will still know where to send it.

2. **Use a Freepost address** if you can afford to (contact Royal Mail for details).

3. **Use a Freephone number**. British Telecom and Mercury both offer this service via their 0800 and 0500 numbers.

4. Consider offering a **credit card facility** if appropriate.

5. **Use a return address** that is as short as possible and easy to spell.

After you have written an advert, put it aside for a day or so. Then return to it and ask yourself: "Is it clear what the reader has to do?" What do you want them to do? For example, do you want them to:

> **TIP**
>
> If you are using coupons in different publications, code the coupon in the bottom corner so you can tell where it was cut out from. That way you can monitor response to your advert, and assess which publication produced the best response, which is essential if you are planning to advertise again. You can do this for radio adverts too. Ask people to write to Department X for one radio station and Department Y for another.

- complete a coupon asking for more information.

- send in a donation.

- call you for details of a product or service.

- telephone your counselling line.

- join your organisation.

- think in a different way about an issue, or change their behaviour (e.g. by boycotting certain goods or companies).

Have you made it easy for them to take the necessary action? If not, look at the list above and see if any of them can help you to help your readers.

ADVERTORIALS

An advertorial is an advertisement that tries to look like editorial. Unlike real editorial, it is paid for. The name comes from combining 'advert' and 'editorial' and it is sometimes known as a 'special feature' or a 'promotional article'. Why bother with an advertorial when you can place a straight advert instead?

Benefits of Advertorials

- straight adverts should ideally be short and punchy. As an advertorial looks very much like a feature article (or even a series of articles spanning several pages), it is a good method for getting a serious or more complex message across.

- there is space to go into detail and to illustrate using a range of photos, graphs, case histories and facts and figures.

- unlike editorial you can, within limits, say what you want to about your organisation, service or campaign.

- sometimes it can be cheaper to buy half a page of advertorial space than the same amount of display advertising space.

Advertorials are definitely on the increase because they have become a good source of revenue for newspapers and magazines. The number of advertorial pages increased by 47% between 1991 and 1992. In the quality press they went from 4 pages in 1991 to 19 in 1992. For the mid-market press the figures rose from 16 to 73, and for the popular press the increase was from nothing to 45.

Different publications approach advertorials in different ways. Most (and certainly the more expensive publications) will get one of their own reporters (or a freelance) to interview you and a feature will then be written about your work or

> **TIP**
> *If you decide to place an advert in a trade publication, ask them if you can have some editorial too. Although few publications will admit to their magazine being advertising-led, in practice you can often secure editorial by placing an advert. It is always worth a try.*

the product/service you wish to promote. You should ensure you get to see this before publication, and to amend it if necessary. They will probably also send a photographer along to take some shots, or they may ask you to supply some quality photographs. Smaller publications may ask you to supply an article, which they may then edit.

If you are asked to write the copy:

- find out how many words are required and by when.

- write in a style that will appeal to the readership (refer to back copies of the publication).

- ensure that you make the article lively and not too introspective

The Ethics of Advertorials

Some people regard advertorials as unethical, for in resembling editorial they are attempting to trick the reader. (An independent survey, however, has revealed that the majority of readers can distinguish among advertisements, advertorials and editorials. However, the same survey found that 8% of respondents said that the information in advertorials was more convincing than information in editorials!) The Periodical Publishers' Association produces guidelines on the labelling of advertorials. The Committee of Advertising Practice also has a guideline that advertisement promotions should be designed and presented in such a way that they can be easily distinguished from editorial. It is a fact, however, that many advertorials do look very much like ordinary features, and even use the same typeface and page layout.

> **TIP**
> You can often get an advert for free by using the listings column in your local free newspaper. Most have a column or diary where they publicise community and charity events, and usually there is no charge for this. They often have a help/request column too, which you can use to advertise for volunteers and helpers.

I personally rarely read advertorials because I know that the chances are that I will not be reading an objective piece. Many journalists share this view and feel that their widespread use erodes a publication's credibility and brings their profession into disrepute. They do, however, have their uses, particularly for organisations that would find it otherwise difficult to attract editorial coverage.

GEARING UP FOR THE ONSLAUGHT

If you place an advert or advertorial, you are doing so in the hope that people will take action. Be ready for them when they do:

- warn your staff, especially your receptionist, that there will be more people than usual calling or writing in.

- take on temporary staff if you anticipate the need, or ensure that you are not light-staffed due to holidays.

- make sure staff are available so calls can be transferred to them.

- ensure that staff know what to say and what details to take down: all calls must be handled professionally.

- have information packs, acknowledgement letters, promotional material etc. ready to be sent out.

- have a distribution/response system in place *before* you place your adverts.

THE MEDIA PLAN

If you are placing a one-off advert, perhaps to publicise an event, there is no need to prepare an advertising (sometimes known as media) plan. However, if advertising is a major part of your promotional work, you should draw up in advance of programme which states:

- what adverts you will be running.

- when.

- where (in which publications/ radio stations).

- at what cost.

- for what effect.

This should be included in your marketing strategy (see Chapter Twelve).

> **TIP**
>
> *If you plan to run a series of different adverts, do not prepare and place the first one before starting work on others in the series. You need to have the whole series produced, or at least well advanced, before the first advert is placed.*
>
> *Adverts need to be seen to be from the same stable, for they rely on the familiarity factor for recognition. You can make it clear that your different adverts are from the same organisation by using a standard layout, the same typefaces in each advert and so on. If each advert looks totally different from the next, you are having to re-establish yourself with each new one. Your aim is to build on the last one, not start from scratch again.*

CHOOSING AND USING AN ADVERTISING AGENCY

If you are planning on doing a lot of advertising, and you do not have an in-house team, you will probably find that you need the services of an advertising agency. They can:

- come up with ideas for adverts that achieve your objectives.

- advise on where, when and how to advertise.

- prepare artwork for you.

- buy advertising space for you.

There are three main types of agency:

1. creative agencies.

2. media independents.

3. full service agencies.

Creatives

These are the agencies that deal with the creative side of advertising. They will come up with clever ideas and do all of the artwork for you. They are 'fee-based'. In other words you agree a fee in advance and they will carry out the work on your brief for that agreed fee. They can do more than straight advertising and will take on the design of corporate identities, exhibitions and other publicity material. (Do not confuse them with graphic designers. Graphic designers will do design work for you, but creative advertising agencies have expertise in advertising that most standard designers do not.)

> **TIP**
> *Select adverts that are designed to be effective, not those that have been produced to win creative awards.*

Media Independents

Media independents specialise in buying space in the media. They do no creative work at all. Because they buy in large volume they can save you money. Media buyers may take as little as two or three per cent commission for buying space for you, which compares favourably with full service agencies. They will not only buy space for you; they will also help you with media planning.

Full Service Agencies

These agencies combine creative teams with in-house media buyers. In other words you get everything you need in the one place. It generally costs more, but it is less hassle to use a one-stop shop and is perhaps the best starting point if you are new to advertising. Full service agencies get an automatic 10 to 15 per cent discount from the media when they buy space. Traditionally this money is used to fund the creative work on big advertising campaigns. However, for small campaigns you will probably have to pay a fee for creative work, planning and the management of your account. Generally full service agencies concentrate on 'above the line' advertising (in the media), though they also offer 'below the line' services such as brochures and other promotional material.

If you can, approach agencies recommended to you by people or organisations you trust. If you don't know anyone who has used an agency, look at charity advertising in the press and contact the organisations who appear to be doing a good job. Ask them which agency they use. This information will be particularly useful, because most agencies specialise in commercial advertising and will probably know very little about charities, so it is important to try to select an agency that already works, or has done so in the past, for a charity or voluntary organisation. With the growth in the number of quangos, local authorities, NHS trusts and voluntary organisations using advertising, finding an agency with relevant experience is easier than it used to be.

Contact at least three agencies and tell them what you are looking for. It is best if you can prepare a written brief (see the sample brief on page 113). This will give the agencies a clear idea of what you hope to achieve. Ask the agencies to let you know whether or not they are interested in your business (some may turn you down because your budget is too small or there is a conflict of interest with another client – e.g. if they handle the advertising account for a cigarette manufacturer and you are an anti-smoking charity, you may get turned away – or, of course, you might decide that you can't do business with them anyway in that case). Set a deadline and ask the selected agencies to get back to you by then with ideas on how they would tackle your campaign.

Look through the submissions and ask in to do a presentation (known as a pitch) those agencies which have impressed you with what they have submitted. Ask them to present to you on their work both generally (known as a credentials presentation) and specifically on how they would approach your assignment and what ideas they have. Get them to bring to the presentation a document setting out their approach and detailing their costs. Alternatively, go to their premises for the presentation; it is more time-consuming, but you get a better idea of who you will be doing business with.

Some agencies will ask you for a fee just for pitching. This is to cover the time and materials involved in preparing ideas for you. It is up to you to decide whether or not you are willing to see agencies who expect payment at this early stage.

Select an agency from those you have seen or, if you are still not sure, draw up a new pitch list and start again.

When assessing the performance of prospective agencies, ask yourself:

- did they fulfil the requirements of the brief in their tender documents?
- was their presentation confident?
- did they come up with good ideas?
- did they seem personally committed or sympathetic to our cause?
- did they seem to understand what we are about?
- did they handle questions well?
- do I feel, from what I have seen, that I have confidence in them?

In addition to telling your prospective consultants about yourself, you need to know about them. Ask them:

- what experience they have of working for organisations similar to your own. Ask for names of clients and examples of their work. Take up references.

- what knowledge and understanding they have of your work. If none of your consultants knows much about your field, ask them how they would go about building up their expertise.

- who will be working on your account. Ask for their CVs, so you can be sure of their experience. (The people who present to you are not always those who will be carrying out the work.)

- how many staff they have.

- how long they have been established.

- what other clients they work for. Is there an actual or potential conflict of interest?

- how they intend to evaluate the success of the work they carry out for you.

- has the agency won any industry awards.

Pick an agency that has relevant experience. If you are doing radio or TV advertising, it is important that your agency has worked in these fields before. Some agencies specialise in press work, and are very good at this, but have limited experience of broadcast advertising. If, however, you are limiting yourself to print advertising, that's fine.

TIP

If you are concerned that your agency may become complacent, let them know that they will be required to take part in a competitive re-pitch for your account every three years. This is common practice and keeps agencies on their toes and ensures that you are getting the best deal.

You might find the sample table below useful for comparing one ad agency with another. Give each agency marks out of ten for each category (replace the given categories with ones that are relevant to your assignment). One is the lowest score and ten the highest. You may decide not to go for the highest overall score, but to opt for an agency that scores well all round. It is up to you.

Sample Table For Evaluating Ad Agencies

CRITERIA	AGENCY 1	AGENCY 2	AGENCY 3
understanding of our needs			
experience in this field			
sympathy to our cause			
creativity and ideas			
approach to the ad campaign			
team involved			
confidence and competence			
total cost			
TOTAL SCORE			

Sample Advertising Brief

THE TOY HOSPITAL
Advertising Campaign Brief

About Us

We are a newly registered national charity. We have just registered with the Charity Commission but as yet we have not had a public launch and therefore no one has heard of us; we have no track record and no profile. We want to launch ourselves using a combination of press advertising and editorial obtained via PR (we have already engaged the services of a PR consultant and would expect our advertising and PR people to work closely together to create a complementary publicity campaign).

We aim to get the public to donate old, unwanted and broken toys to us. (A national supermarket chain has agreed to have collection points in each of its stores.) We will refurbish the toys and give them free of charge to children whose parents could otherwise not afford them. We need from the public both toys and the money necessary to refurbish them. We also need volunteers to clean and repair toys and deliver them to needy families. Additionally we must attract finance to cover our running costs and to pay the salaries of our four full-time staff. Thanks to a legacy we have enough to cover our launch costs and to keep the charity going for six months. It is therefore urgent that we orchestrate a high profile launch (launch date is May 1st and Blue Peter have agreed to cover our story on that day) backed up with powerful advertising.

Our Advertising Objectives

1. **To inform the public about our work.** We will commission market research eight weeks after the first adverts appear and we expect name recognition in 65% of our sample and an understanding of our work in 40% of those interviewed.

2. **To get the public to donate toys.** We expect the first toys to be handed into our collection depots on the day the first adverts appear – launch day. By the end of the first month we expect to have collected 50,000 toys.

3. **To attract donations.** As a direct result of the press adverts we expect to get £100,000 in donations by two months after launch date.

Initially we are looking for a set of one-off advertisements to launch the charity and meet the above objectives. Assuming we are successful, we shall be looking to build upon the initial push by developing a rolling advertising programme to maintain awareness and interest.

Our Audience

Our adverts need to be aimed at the widest possible public. American research shows that it is not just children and their parents who give, although they are the main donors, along with schools and Brownies/Scouts (there is a similar charity operating across the Atlantic). Cash donations come also from childless couples and grandparents, who are the main donors in terms of the amounts they give.

Our Budget

Our advertising budget of £75,000 must cover all media space and all creative work, project management etc. We are aware that this is relatively small, given what we are hoping to achieve, but remember that advertising will be backed up by PR and by displays in supermarkets across Britain.

LEGAL, DECENT, HONEST AND TRUTHFUL?

All advertising must be legal, decent, honest and truthful. The Advertising Standards Authority (ASA) is the independent body responsible for ensuring that advertising meets the standard and is in the public interest. It has the power to investigate complaints about advertisements, and has investigated many about charity advertising. Indeed in 1995 it criticised many charities for being "over-zealous" and for "overstepping the line between presenting a possibly distressing, but accurate, picture of their cause and misinforming people about an issue by exaggerating or stretching the truth".

If you are a campaigning charity, chances are that your 'opposition' will want to catch you out as often as possible. They will be carefully monitoring your advertising for any breaches and will report you with great speed. Friends of the Earth ran a cinema advert showing a toilet with a mahogany seat overflowing with blood. The voice-over talked about Brazilian Indians who own mahogany trees paying with their lives if they refuse to sell the trees. Complaints were received by the ASA from the Timber Trade Federation and the Brazilian Embassy.

Remember that you can be in breach unintentionally – it is not just unethical businesses trying to mislead the public who have complaints against them upheld. In the ASA's monthly report for October 1995, Friends of the Earth, Greenpeace, NSPCC and the International Fund for Animal Welfare had complaints against them upheld. Make sure that any claims you make in your adverts can be substantiated. The NSPCC ran a Saatchi & Saatchi-designed billboard campaign which read: "One in every eight people who walk past this poster was abused as a child." When the inevitable complaints followed, the NSPCC was able to produce independent research to back their claims. However, when they screened a cinema advert showing an unborn baby in the womb reacting to an argument between its parents, the charity could not demonstrate that a foetus can be emotionally disturbed by the hostility around it.

TRUE STORY: GETTING IT WRONG

The International Fund for Animal Welfare advertised in the national press for donations. Their advert was headed: "To you, it's a pet. To a Korean, it's a bowl of soup." It continued: "Thanks to campaigning from IFAW and its supporters, the South Korean government now has an Animal Protection Act. Regrettably, it's not being enforced. And cats are still being slaughtered at the rate of around 400,000 a year; either butchered, hammered to death, or even boiled to death with herbs to make 'medicinal' soup." The Advertising Standards Authority received a number of complaints that it was offensive to imply that Koreans viewed cats only as an ingredient for soup, and that the 400,000 figure could not be substantiated. The ASA obtained expert advice and concluded that Koreans regarded cats as pets rather than food and that a significant part of the population of South Korea was Buddhist and therefore vegetarian. The complaint was upheld. A potentially powerful advertisement from a charity doing good work fell foul of the Code of Practice and had to be withdrawn.

TRUE STORY: GETTING IT RIGHT

The RSPCA ran four hard-hitting adverts in the national press. They showed how hunting leads to the death of domestic pets as well as wild animals and how the law offers little protection to animals. One, for example, had a headline: "Wild animals aren't the only victims of hunting" and this was illustrated by a photograph of the stuffed head of a cat mounted on a sporting trophy. It read: "You won't see this kind of trophy hanging in a country house because it's illegal ... yet every year pets are ripped apart by hunting dogs and garrotted by wire snares ..." Nearly 100 complaints were received from across Britain, presumably orchestrated by the pro-hunting lobby. The RSPCA was able to provide documentary evidence to support each of their claims and so the complaints against them were not upheld.

The ASA recognises the problems charities face and has said: "Limited resources and accountability to supporters means that charities are under particular pressure to produce advertising that makes people sit up and take notice. Those creating such campaigns feel that they weaken their impact if they have to qualify claims or state opinions rather than fact." The Committee of Advertising Practice (see below) offers free pre-publication advice to help organisations operate within the Code of Practice. The ASA says that often small changes to copy can make the difference between fact and fiction without a charity losing the force of its message.

The Committee of Advertising Practice (CAP) is the self-regulatory body that devises and enforces the British Codes of Advertising and Sales Promotion. They produce a really useful guide to the codes, which is available free of charge (see address section). CAP also offer a free and confidential advice service to advertisers, to help ensure that they do not fall foul of the Codes. Ring 0171-580 4100 and ask for the copy advice team.

The Codes apply to adverts in newspapers, magazines, catalogues, mailings, brochures and posters, but not to broadcast commercials on radio and TV. These are policed by the Independent Television Commission and the Radio Authority. A full copy of the Codes is available, and you should ensure that you get hold of one if you are planning any advertising. The main points that apply to charities are:

1. all adverts should be legal, decent, honest and truthful.

2. all adverts should be prepared with a sense of responsibility to consumers and society.

3. advertisers must hold documentary evidence to prove all claims that are capable of objective substantiation.

4. if there is a significant division of informed opinion about any claims made, they should not be portrayed as universally agreed.

5. no advert should cause fear or distress without good reason. Advertisers should not use shocking claims or images merely to attract attention.

6. when it comes to political advertising, the identity and status of such advertisers should be clear. If their address or other

contact details are not generally available they should be included in the advert.

'Political' Advertising

The Broadcasting Act 1990 was introduced to deny extremists such as the National Front access to the mass media. Its effect has been to prevent many charities' adverts from being seen and heard. In 1995 Amnesty International was banned from airing a radio advert which urged listeners to "break the silence about human rights violations." This was regarded as a political advert and was banned by the Radio Authority. Amnesty appealed to the High Court, which upheld the ruling. However, a TV advert by Survival International had its ban lifted. Before making an advert for broadcast, ensure it does not fall foul of the Act.

Don't Exploit or Patronise

A few years ago most aid charities used images of Third World people that many now regard as patronising, even racist. Black people stared out from adverts, hungry and poor, waiting for help and assistance from the affluent West. They were portrayed as hapless victims, passive and defenceless. Some people feel that this kind of advertising has created a negative image of the Third World, and that the many positive things happening in Third World countries, and indeed the very reasons for Third World underdevelopment, are underplayed or ignored.

Organisations working for people with physical and mental disabilities have also been on the receiving end of criticism, much of it coming from disabled people. The recipients of the charity have in the past (and are still, by some organisations) been portrayed as helpless victims rather than as normal individuals who face particular difficulties because of their disability.

Charities do face a dilemma. Do you exploit imagery on the grounds that the ends justify the means, or do you take the view that advertising should be used to challenge perceptions, not to confirm prejudices and ignorance? A clever ad campaign was run by a cerebral palsy charity. Billboard and newspaper adverts showed a photograph of a mother with her disabled son. The caption said something like: "My son has a learning age of 12 ... he's only ten. The advertising was part of a much wider marketing effort to alter and update the image of a charity that previously had a rather old-fashioned image.

WHAT'S THE DAMAGE?

It is impossible to say exactly what you will need to pay to place an advert. For press advertising, factors affecting price include:

- **time of year:** there are slack periods when you can get a better deal.

- **size:** the larger your advert, the costlier it will be.

- **circulation of publication:** larger circulation generally means a higher price, though it also means that your advert is reaching more people.

- **situation:** an advert on the front page is more expensive than one on the back.

- **colour:** black and white is cheaper than colour, and 'spot colour' (adding a splash of red to your black and white advert, for example) is cheaper than full colour.

- **how you buy space:** whether you go direct or via a media buyer (a specialist who buys media space and can get quite good deals, though generally only for fairly large ad campaigns).

For broadcast adverts, the price depends on:

- which station/network (some are more costly than others, depending on the area they cover, the listening/viewing figures).

- time of day (or night).

- during/after which programme the advert is aired.

Advertising departments produce 'rate cards' which set out the cost of adverts according to size, position and so on. Often rates are negotiable, so do try to get the official rate reduced.

> **TIP**
> If you are planning to place a series of adverts in the same publication, you can generally negotiate a discount.

If you want up-to-date guidelines on current rates, go to your public library and consult British Rate and Data (BRAD), a publication which lists all the UK's advertising media, their rates and their readership.

MONITORING AND EVALUATION

When you place an advertisement, keep a log of enquiries so that you can see where's best to advertise. This will be invaluable should you decide to re-run an advertising campaign, for you will be able to see at a glance whether Publication A or Radio Station B came up with the goods. The sample log on the next page can be adapted to suit your purposes.

Prepare an analysis of your logs. Refer to the sample analysis on page 119 to see what facts you could draw out.

Once your campaign has ended, you should sit down with your log and your objectives and take a look at whether or not you have been successful. Another measure of success (in addition to your objectives) is to look at income and expenditure. If you have spent a great deal more on your adverts than you have received in donations or subscriptions, perhaps you have failed. On the other hand, if one of your objectives was to build up a database of interested people, and your campaign has achieved this, perhaps you can claim success.

	Caller's name and address	Saw advert in (publication)	Requested more info (tick if applicable)	Made donation (amount)
		Sample advertising response log		
1.	Jane Smith 77 Duke Street Arpton AR1 1BB	Guardian	✗	£10 (credit card)
2.	Gordon King 1 Queen Street Liston L12 1PT	Times	✔	no
3.				
4.				
5.				
6.				
7.				
8.				
9.				
10.				
11.				
12.				

Sample Advertising Response Log Analysis

MUSIC THERAPY FOR BLIND CHILDREN APPEAL:
Analysis Of Advertising Campaign

THE FACTS

The main findings of the analysis of the log sheets are:

- we received 600 donations, 50% from the Guardian advert, 14% from Classic FM Radio and 36% from The Times.

- in total we received £25,000 in donations.

- although Times readers represented only 36% of enquirers, they gave in total £12,500 (half of all money raised).

- the average donation was £42.

- the median donation was £38.

- as a direct result of the information packs sent out, 107 people so far have taken out Deeds of Covenant. This will represent an income of £10,000 for the charity over three years.

- Guardian readers were more generous when it came to covenants: 75% of all covenants came from them.

THE CONCLUSIONS

1. Our experiment with radio did not work well, producing relatively few donations and covenants. We failed to cover our costs and I recommend that we concentrate future efforts on press advertising.

2. While on the face of it The Times appears to have produced most money up-front, it produced fewer enquiries and less in covenants. Nevertheless, the amounts given were above average and it could be useful in the future for one-off appeals. It was, however, more expensive to advertise in.

3. The Guardian has come up trumps in terms of long-term income from covenants. We have a better chance of developing a relationship with covenanters than we have with one-off donors. Also, the cost of advertising in The Guardian was less than The Times, so all in all it appears to have been the best option.

HAVE A GO YOURSELF

Read through the following advertisement, which has been written for the national press, and itemise what is wrong with it.

DOVERSTONE DONKEY SANCTUARY

In the 1920s there were no donkey sanctuaries in Britain, but then a donkey-lover by the name of Mr Donald Key founded Britain's very first donkey sanctuary in Bournton. Since that time donkey sanctuaries have sprung up across Britain, run by a range of charities dedicated to the needs of elderly and retired donkeys. The Doverstone Donkey Sanctuary is one such charity, founded in 1991 by Mrs Maria Hee-Haw OBE, who most generously left in her will the handsome sum of £100,000. This has been used to establish the Doverstone Donkey Sanctuary, which has gone from strength to strength and now attracts an income of over £500,000 a year. This month the Sanctuary launches its 'Adopt a Donkey' scheme. It will enable people to adopt a donkey for just £5 a year. Subscribers will receive a photograph of their donkey, a copy of its family tree and history, and a twice-yearly update on how the donkey is faring.

If you would like to adopt a donkey, write to the following address with your details and enclose a cheque for £5: Mr Steven Reid-Cross CBE, Honorary Secretary, Adopt a Donkey Scheme, The Doverstone Donkey Sanctuary, Donkey House, 27 Green Lane, Doverstone DS12 0BZ.

Discussion

The material contained in the advert is potentially very good, but so many mistakes have been made in the way it is written and presented that it is not likely to be a very effective advert.

- it is a national charity, even though it is based in Doverstone, but because of the way the advert is presented, it comes across as local. By mentioning the network of donkey sanctuaries across Britain, it is almost encouraging readers to support their local one, not this one.

- the advert is not about donkey sanctuaries, though you could be forgiven for thinking so. It is about adopting donkeys. In other words, the advert is selling the organisation, not the brand. It is the equivalent to an advert for Heinz that attempts to sell Heinz rather than baked beans.

- responding to the offer is made too complicated. First you have to write in; there is no simple coupon. Next you have to fill out a long return address, then you have to contact them to find out to whom the cheque should be made. Could you be bothered?

- its headline is not designed to attract attention and encourage the reader to read on.

- it contains too much irrelevant background information and facts.

- it fails to exploit the reader's interest in donkeys by throwing in an emotive appeal.

- the copy is dull.

- by writing in the third person the copy is less appealing.

- by mentioning its endowment of £100,000 and its annual income of £500,000 it sounds as if it is doing quite well and does not need the help of the reader. There is no sense in the advert of urgent need, or of how the money will be spent.

ADOPT A DONKEY FOR THE PRICE OF SOME CARROTS!

Some donkeys have put a lifetime into working to serve humans, but now they find themselves abandoned and alone. You can adopt a donkey for just £5, enabling us to give it a home, shelter, good food, exercise and the company of other retired donkeys.

Helping donkeys in need

As well as the good feeling of knowing that you are helping a donkey in need, your membership of our Adopt a Donkey scheme buys you a photo of your adopted donkey, its family tree and an account of the life of your very own donkey. You'll even get a progress report twice a year.

Our donkeys urgently need your support, so please adopt a donkey today.

I want to adopt a donkey. Find enclosed my cheque for £5. (If you can afford more than £5, your extra help can help provide new facilities at our new donkey sanctuary.)

Name _____

Address _____

_____

**Cheques made payable to Adopt a Donkey should be sent to:
PO Box 4, Doverstone DS12 0BZ.**

IN1

Discussion

This is much better because:

- the headline attracts attention and is intriguing.

■ a sub heading is used, which helps encourage the glancer to become a reader.

■ it is written in the first person, which gives it more appeal.

■ it appeals to the reader direct.

■ it quantifies what help costs (a £5 bag of carrots).

■ it offers readers the chance to give more if they wish, without making anyone feel mean if they can't.

■ it has a coupon response to make replying easier.

■ the copy stresses the urgency of the appeal, encouraging people to act.

■ it cuts out unnecessary background material and detail.

■ it uses emotive words, such as 'abandoned', 'alone' and 'in need' which are designed to appeal to donkey-lovers.

■ the return address is much shorter, making it easy to reply.

■ the coupon is coded, so the charity can evaluate the success of the adverts it placed, enabling it to work out which newspapers and which days were most effective.

CHAPTER NINE
PROMOTION –
PUBLIC RELATIONS

What's in this chapter?

■ *the difference between advertising and public relations.*

■ *how to write an effective news release.*

■ *how to exploit media contacts for news and feature coverage.*

■ *how to organise news conferences to promote your service or charity.*

■ *how to set up a photocall.*

In the last chapter we looked at media coverage obtained through paid-for advertising. You don't have to use advertising to achieve coverage in the media. Public relations techniques can help you secure some first class exposure. You can use public relations techniques to attract editorial coverage on radio, television and in the press. This can be a superb way of promoting your organisation, a new service, a fundraising appeal or a campaign. It can raise awareness and your profile, promote your work, persuade, reach a wide audience, influence, raise funds and attract support. And best of all, PR-generated coverage is usually cheaper to obtain than advertising coverage. But what is the difference between PR-generated coverage and advertising?

IS ADVERTISING THE SAME AS PR?

Not everyone is clear about the difference between media coverage secured by advertising, and editorial that results from public relations' efforts. Essentially, editorial coverage secured by PR is not paid for, while advertisements are.

Pros of advertising over PR

■ advertising is much more controllable than PR.

■ unlike PR, your coverage is guaranteed; it is not left to chance.

■ you decide on the wording.

■ you decide on the publication.

■ you decide on the photographs or illustrations.

■ you decide on the timing.

■ you decide on the position in the publication (e.g. front page, top of page 4).

■ you decide on the size of the coverage (e.g. full page, quarter page).

■ you decide whether to go for full colour, spot colour or black and white.

Cons of advertising over PR

■ cost is a major drawback.

■ editorial coverage carries more weight than advertising because it is regarded as more impartial.

Pros of PR over advertising

■ it is generally cheaper.

■ you can potentially get coverage in lots of publications for little more than the cost of a stamp.

■ statements made via editorial are more likely to be believed than statements made in adverts, so it can be a very persuasive tool.

■ an article is less likely to be ignored than an advert.

■ it is a really affordable way of getting on TV and radio.

Cons of PR

■ you cannot guarantee coverage.

■ you have no control over where or when your coverage appears.

■ your news release may be edited or distorted.

■ you have no control over the wording of the story that finally appears; it might take a very different line to the one you had hoped for, perhaps leading to damaging or negative coverage.

CAN PR HELP YOU PROMOTE YOUR PRODUCT?

'Public relations' is often equated with 'media relations'. In fact PR involves a host of different things, media relations (i.e. getting free coverage for your product or service in the media) being just one of them, albeit a very important one.

A lot of people still believe that news gets into the media thanks to the efforts of journalists beavering away uncovering news. In fact many of the stories you read in newspapers or hear about on the radio or television are placed there by PR consultants acting for central and local government, companies and charities. But how? It is possible to get media coverage for your services in five main ways:

1. the chief method is via something called a 'news release'. A news release is a news story which has been set out in a particular style (see below).

2. by holding a news conference or event.

3. by setting up a feature.

4. by setting up a photocall.

5. by talking to media contacts.

We will look at each in turn, starting with news releases.

NEWS RELEASES

Many newspapers, and radio and TV stations, rely on news releases for a fair amount of their output. Good releases (i.e. well written, properly presented, well timed and with a strong story line) will often be used verbatim. Even photographs accompanying releases are sometimes used (though obviously not by radio and television).

Your aim is to write a news release that promotes your service or product and is, at the same time, a 'good read'.

Journalists hate receiving what they dismissively term 'PR puffery' – releases over-selling a product and using exaggerated claims and hyperbole. These releases end up not in the newspaper, but in the wastepaper bucket. You need to find something about your product or service that is newsworthy if you are to stand any chance of its being used. Fortunately you have a head start over commercial companies. Most of the stories they try to 'sell' to the media are too blatantly commercial; the media is not in the game of free advertising. On the other hand, many of the products and services offered by charities and voluntary organisations are of interest to the media. A TV station would be unlikely to run a story on a new commercial business centre, but it would probably broadcast a feature on a business centre set up to help unemployed school-leavers find work or training. Stories with a social edge are generally stronger than stories with a hard commercial one. So while companies might have the advantage of a large PR budget, you will probably have better stories to offer the media.

If you are launching a new product or service, enhancing an existing one, or have some other news, you have an opportunity of gaining some good coverage in the media – so long as you can produce an interesting release with genuine news value.

Ten Tips for Release-Writing

1. Capture the news editor's attention in the first paragraph by leading with a newsworthy angle; if you don't, your release will be binned within seconds.

2. Include all the relevant information early on in your release, by covering 'The Five Ws'. These stand for:

What – what is happening? what is being launched? what is the new service?

Who – who will be doing it? who will be doing the launch/opening?

When – when is it happening?

Where – where will the service/launch be?

Why – why is the service/product being launched/expanded?

3. Include a quote in your release from a named person. If the newspaper uses your release, it will appear to their readers that they actually interviewed you, when really they just printed your release.

4. Keep it brief and stick to the point – ideally one page and preferably no more than two.

5. Avoid jargon and hyperbole.

6. Date your release so that it is clear that it is current.

7. Include at least one contact name and number and ensure the contact is available, easy to get hold of, and fully briefed.

8. Also include a home number so that you can be contacted outside office hours.

9. If you need to send background briefing material, do so on a separate sheet (not part of the main release).

10. Write your release so that it can be chopped paragraph by paragraph from the bottom up, and still make sense.

You can see overleaf an example of a news release, illustrating layout as well as presenting an interesting storyline of the sort that the media would be interested in. On the subject of layout, there is a convention about how releases should be laid out on the page.

Getting Your Looks Right

To maximise your chances of getting your release used, make sure that your release looks right:

- **double space** releases – so reporters have space to scribble comments and edit.

- use **wide margins** – for the same reasons.

- keep them **single sided** – for ease of reading.

- make sure your release is **typed**. Hand-written releases are too difficult to read and look unprofessional.

- use **plain paper** for continuation sheets, but your headed notepaper for the top one (unless you have specially-printed news release paper).

sample news release

BRAINWAVES
210 Towngate Street, Edinthorpe. Tel. 01884 123456

NEWS RELEASE

For immediate use
Thursday, April 11 1996

ROCK STAR TONY TINSEL LAUNCHES PIONEERING SCHEME FOR YOUNG PEOPLE WITH BRAIN INJURIES

A pioneering scheme for young people with brain injuries, the first of its kind is Britain, was launched in Edinthorpe today (Thursday) by rock star Tony Tinsel, who has himself suffered from a brain injury.

'BrainBusters', a new rehabilitation programme for young brain-injured people, is run by Brainwaves. It has been devised to meet the particular needs of younger people who have suffered a brain injury as the result of a motorcycle or car crash, sports or play accident. Previously there was no provision anywhere in the country specifically for young people.

Rock idol Tony Tinsel, who last year suffered a brain injury after diving into a swimming pool, launched the new service. He said: "I know how isolated you can feel when you have suffered a brain injury. Young people often find themselves cut off from their friends, and as a result can miss out on many of the fun things that teenagers do. This scheme will bring together young people and give them a chance not only to socialise, but to learn to cope with their injury and rebuild their lives."

Brainwaves is a registered charity based in the Towngate area of town. The BrainBusters rehabilitation sessions will be run from the charity's offices, and youngsters between the ages of 14 and 19 will be referred to the service via their GPs.

The £50,000 funding for the service came jointly from Edinthorpe Health Commission and Edinthorpe Council.

ends

For further information contact:

Dominic Duckworth, Director of Brainwaves	Andrea Grant, Chair
Day 01884 12345	Day 01884 99015
Evening 01884 44567	Evening 01884 67656

- don't **format** – i.e. avoid bold, italics, capitals etc. in the body text.

- don't **split** a sentence from one page to the next. Ideally, don't let a paragraph continue over the page.

- **staple pages together** - so your top sheet does not lose its companion in a busy newsroom.

It is best not to send the same release to everyone. The needs and interests of your local newspaper will be different from those of a national paper, which will in turn be different to what a radio station might be interested in. Amend releases slightly according to whom they are being sent to. You might want to include local information for a local paper, but omit it in the version for the nationals, for example.

What Will Happen to Your Release?

When a newspaper receives your release, they will do one of the following:

- use it verbatim or edit it a little.

- call you for further information, and add this to the story.

- bin it – perhaps because it is no good, irrelevant for their readership, arrived too late, or because they had too much news already.

When a television or radio station gets your release and wishes to cover your story, they may:

- ask you to the studio for a live or recorded interview.

- do a recorded or live interview down the telephone (generally radio only) or

- do their own news report based on your release, possibly following a brief, informal chat with you on the telephone.

- send a reporter (and film crew, if it is TV) to you.

Where Should You Send Your Releases?

Most of the time you will know where to send your release – the local media, for example, or your own trade publications. There may be times, though, when you need to reach out to other publications or programmes that you are not at all familiar with. There are a number of easy-to-use directories which can help you, listing trade, technical and consumer titles, local papers, TV and radio, national media, European media, and business publications. You can find out what publications (or programmes) cover your audience or issue, the names of the editor and any special correspondents; addresses, telephone and fax numbers; circulation details; frequency of publication. They are available by subscription (though they are expensive) but you may find that your local reference library has one or more. Various titles are available, but the best known are: PR Planner UK; PIMS United Kingdom Media Directory; Editors; Benn's. Some are also available on disk and CD ROM.

NEWS CONFERENCES AND MEDIA EVENTS

Releases are generally the best, easiest and most cost-effective way of using the media to promote a new service or product. There are, however, times when it is preferable to talk to the media face-to-face rather than by using a page of A4. On such occasions (such as when your story is fairly complex or especially newsworthy), you can either hold a news conference or host a media event.

News conferences (often called 'press conferences') are a lot of hard work to organise, so only hold one if you have good reason. You might, for example, be launching a controversial new service (a free condom scheme for prostitutes, for example) and believe that it is better to face the media than issue a news release that cannot get across the emotion in the same way as you could in person.

Ten Golden Rules

1. Start and finish on time.

2. Say what you have to say as succinctly as possible and then throw it open to questions. Don't ramble on and bore everyone.

3. The best starting time is around 10.30/11am.

4. Speakers at the top table should have name plates before them which can be seen from a distance.

5. Issue guests with name badges.

6. Check your venue for power points for TV crews to use. (They may not always need them, so it is not absolutely essential.)

7. Set aside a quiet side room at your venue for radio interviews to take place.

8. Be available both before and after the news conference (and possibly even the day before) for radio or TV reporters who cannot attend at the time you have scheduled.

9. Be as helpful as you can at accommodating the needs of the media if you want to build a good relationship and maximise coverage.

10. make parking available if you can, try to find a central venue, and send maps if your venue is at all off the beaten track.

Whether you are planning a news conference or organising a newsworthy event, you will need to let the media know in advance of your plans so that they can slot it into their schedule. Send them an invitation, ideally about a week before your event/news conference.

MEDIA INVITATIONS

You can see a sample media invitation on the next page. The key things to know about invitations are:

1. keep them brief.

2. include a paragraph explaining the purpose of the event/news conference and describing what will happen at it.

3. list all the necessary information – start times, venue, speakers etc.

Remember that media invitations are designed to attract reporters to your event, not to take the place of a news release. Don't give too much away in your invitation, just enough to get people there.

FEATURES

Sometimes you can promote a new service by arranging for a feature in the press or on TV or radio. The example given above would work well as feature material. A reporter could talk to brain injured people, including the celebrity, about what it is like, how it affects you, what can be done to help etc. and this could be backed up with facts and figures, information about the new service, quotes from key staff at the charity and so on. If you are launching a service or product that lends itself well to a feature, start by deciding on the best place for it. Radio or TV? Or the press? Which paper? When? It is often best to approach just one publication (or programme) and to offer them an exclusive feature which they can run on the day of the launch. Write briefly to the Features Editor in the first instance, outlining your ideas. Follow this up a week later with a call to assess interest.

PHOTOCALLS

There are three ways of getting photographic coverage for a new service:

1. arrange a photocall and invite photographers.

2. ensure that you have a photo-opportunity as part of your press conference or event, and invite photographers to that.

sample media invitation

BRAINWAVES
210 Towngate Street, Edinthorpe. Tel. 01884 123456

FOR OPERATIONAL USE ONLY:
NOT FOR PUBLICATION OR BROADCAST

INVITATION TO NEWS AND PICTURE EDITORS

ROCK STAR TONY TINSEL TO LAUNCH PIONEERING SCHEME FOR YOUNG PEOPLE WITH BRAIN INJURIES

A pioneering £50,000 scheme for young people with brain injuries, the first of its kind in Britain, will be launched in Edinthorpe by rock star Tony Tinsel, who has himself suffered from a brain injury.

Tony Tinsel, Dominic Duckworth (director of Brainwaves, the charity which will run the new scheme), and brain-injured youngsters will be available for interview and photographs.

You are invited to send a representative

Time: 10.30am

Date: Thursday, April 11 1996

Venue: Brainwaves, Towngate House, 210 Towngate Street, Edinthorpe

For further information contact:

Dominic Duckworth, Director of Brainwaves

Day   01884 12345

Evening   01884 44567

3. send to a newspaper your own photographs with a news release, but make sure that the quality is really good (by using a freelance press photographer who knows what is expected). Remember that national papers are extremely unlikely to use submitted photographs, though local and trade papers are happy to.

Write to picture editors saying when, where, and what photographs can be taken, but only if you have something photogenic on offer. People sitting round tables, 'grip 'n' grins' (people clutching flowers, cheques, certificates etc. and grinning manically) and other dull ideas will not be considered by a newspaper, so be creative and go for a photo-opportunity with flair. Here are some real life examples that attracted lots of media exposure:

- a pressure group opposed to arms sales to totalitarian regimes hired a tank to make a protest at the AGM of a High Street bank which it claimed helped to finance these deals. Large photos of the stunt appeared in the national press and it was covered by television.

- a Scottish charity was given £50,000 by the Post Office to refurbish a derelict building. It organised a photocall outside the building with a giant replica stamp for the value of £50,000. The stamp displayed an artist's impression of the refurbished building. It got into the press and on to TV.

- a London housing charity wanted to publicise the scandal of the capital's empty properties. It refurbished a room in a derelict house as a 'show house' and invited the cameras (TV and press) to see it.

TIP

If you can, time your events or releases for a Sunday, as little news happens then. You might have noticed how Monday's papers are often quite thin, and this is why. Newspapers have staff working on Sundays in order to produce Monday's paper, although the day tends to be a fairly quiet one in the newsroom.

USING CONTACTS

I have assumed here that you have no existing relationship with the media. If you have, and know reporters well, this can be a really good way of getting positive, intelligent coverage. Rather than going through the formality of issuing a news release, you might find it easier and quicker to pick up the phone and chat to a friendly reporter about your new product or service.

For fuller details of how to use the media, and information on other PR techniques, get hold of a copy of The DIY Guide to Public Relations, published by the Directory of Social Change.

CHAPTER TEN

PROMOTION – DIRECT MAIL

What's in this chapter?

■ *the benefits and drawbacks of direct mail.*

■ *how to do test mailings.*

■ *objective-setting and evaluation.*

■ *hiring or building up a mailing list.*

■ *databases and the Data Protection Act.*

■ *envelopes and enclosures.*

■ *making it easy to respond.*

■ *the hidden costs.*

■ *direct advertising.*

Direct mail is marketing jargon for advertising by post. It is the third largest advertising medium in Britain and, according to figures, it is growing all the time. You need only look at the heap of so-called 'junk mail' landing on your doormat daily to be aware of that! Charities have long used the humble letter as a way of attracting donations, but charity direct mail is now a great deal more sophisticated. Just look at the quality of the material you receive from good causes and compare it with what was sent out a few years ago.

In 1993 7.5% of all direct mail was sent by charities. Greenpeace alone sends over a million mailshots every year in Britain and describes direct mail as its "lifeblood. Without it, Greenpeace would not be able to fundraise effectively. As a result, it would not function." Over 80% of Greenpeace's UK fundraising expenditure is on direct marketing and more than 90% of their supporters are recruited through it.

You can use direct mail:

■ to sell e.g. charity Christmas cards or promotional items.

■ to inform e.g. to ensure that people know about a particular issue that they might otherwise not be aware of.

■ to send out postal questionnaires.

■ to encourage people to join your organisation.

■ to seek donations.

■ to campaign – encouraging like-minded people to support your campaign and take action.

There are, of course, both pros and cons with direct mail, which are summarised below:

Benefits of Using Direct Mail

■ if your mailing list is good, direct mail is a great way of targeting those who are potentially interested, and thus of cutting down on wasted effort.

■ it can be cheaper than other forms of advertising/promotion, such as TV or national newspaper advertising, as it is more targeted.

■ it can be used by very small charities, unlike TV and national press advertising.

■ it is harder for other charities to monitor your activities when you use direct mail; unlike press advertising, your message is not slapped across the page for all to see.

■ small mailings can be organised at fairly short notice, so it is a good medium to use where urgency is required, for example when a charity needs to raise funds following a sudden natural disaster.

■ it can be used for test mailings i.e. by sending one mailing to half your list and a different one to the other half, in order to see which approach was more effective (see below).

■ you can get across a lot more information than in a press advert, for example, and can also include enclosures.

■ it is as good for small, locally based charities as it is for large national ones.

■ it is easy to measure response to the mailing.

■ mailings can be personalised to the recipient.

■ the message can be timed to arrive on a particular day or time of year, so it is ideal for seasonal fundraising, such as Christmas mailings (when people are feeling more generous).

Drawbacks of Direct Mail

■ it has a poor image.

■ the hidden costs can be quite high – in addition to the postage costs you need to add production costs of the mailing (including design, envelopes, updating or buying a mailing list etc.).

■ unless your mailing list is up to date, you can waste money mailing to people who have moved away.

- unless your mailing list is made up of the right profile, your cost per enquiry might be too high to justify.

- it is unsolicited so it might not be welcomed by the recipients. Some people hate 'junk' mail and bin it unopened.

TEST MAILINGS

One big advantage of direct mail is that it enables test mailings to be carried out. You can systematically change various elements of your mailing, and monitor the responses to the different mailings. This approach could, for example, help you discover what sort of covering letter or enclosures produce the best results. Do you get a better response when you suggest an amount of money for donors to give, or when you leave it open? A test mailing could help you find out. Does an incentive such as a free badge or bird box make a difference to the quantity and quality of responses to your membership drive? Again, use a test mailing to help you discover.

> **TIP**
> *When doing a test mailing, do not introduce more than one variable in each test. Otherwise you will not know which factor led to increased or decreased response. Remember, though, that you can run several test mailings simultaneously.*

Test Matrices

You can split your mailing to try out different things at the same time. For example, let's say you wanted to try a new mailing list (List X) and to test its performance against the mailing list you usually use (List Y). You also want to see whether offering a free wildlife wallchart will increase subscriptions to your environmental magazine. And you want to know whether reducing the cost of subscription is more effective than offering an incentive. Your test matrix would look like this:

	List Y (usual list)	List X (new list)
Usual pack (control)	A	B
Wallchart incentive	A1	
Lower price subscription	A2	

To find out whether your new list was better than your existing list, you would need to compare the results of A with B. This is done using a control, namely, your standard mailing pack. However, you also want to find out whether other factors affect response. Comparing the results of A1 and A2 will tell you whether the wallchart was more of an incentive than the lower subscription rate.

You can carry on testing until you find the most successful combination of factors. To know which mailings are more successful, you need to code the response device. You can do this by writing or

TRUE STORY

Greenpeace did a split mailing to test what type of message would recruit more supporters. A message about the work of Greenpeace in general outperformed a pack that focused on just one aspect of the organisation's work. In another test a manila envelope was used alongside a white one. The manila outperformed the white by 94%.

printing a code (e.g. M1, M2 or M3) on the coupon or form that the respondent returns to you.

DON'T RUSH INTO IT

As with so many things, a direct mail campaign should not be undertaken on the spur of the moment. It should be a part of your overall marketing strategy. You need to be sure that it is the right method, you need to establish what you hope to get out of it, and you need to evaluate the campaign at the end. Charities have been criticised for their use of direct mail, both by recipients of the mail and by direct mail professionals. Brann, in his book Cost-effective Direct Marketing, said: "There are few areas of direct response promotion which use direct mail as ineffectively as do some charities." If you want to ensure that you are not one of the charities that he was thinking of, ensure that you ask the following questions before setting off down the direct market road:

SETTING OBJECTIVES FOR A DIRECT MAIL CAMPAIGN

The first question you need to ask is **what**. What do you hope to achieve from a direct mail campaign? Be as specific as you can. In other words, it is not sufficient to say: "To attract more donations". You need to quantify, for example, "To attract 100 new members and £100,000 in donations" or "To attract 300 enquiries and to turn half of the enquirers into members within six months".

Question two is **who**. Who is your target audience? Who do you plan to write to? Again be specific. It is no good saying "People likely to support us". You need to say "People in the south east of England who have in the past made a donation to an environmental charity".

Finally you must ask **how**. How will your direct mailing fit into your organisation's marketing work? Will it just be a one-off mailing, one of a series, a mailing backed up by other activity such as PR or press advertising? A mailing to back up other activity? You need to view your mailing in context.

Direct Mail Fact File

- ■ in 1989, 80% of consumer direct mail was opened and 61% was read.
- ■ by 1993, 83% was opened and 68% read.
- ■ charity direct mail campaigns increased by 16% from 1994 to 1995.
- ■ women are more likely than men to open direct mail.

- charity direct mail accounts for 18% of all consumer direct mail campaigns.

- in 1989 in social grade AB, 76% of people opened direct mail.

- this had risen to 82% by 1993.

- in 1989 in social grade DE, 90% of people opened direct mail.

- this had dropped to 82% by 1993.

- nearly 1,800 different direct mail campaigns were issued by UK charities between August 1994 and July 1995.

MAILING LISTS

There are two factors that make or break a direct mailing campaign:

1. the mailing pack.
2. the mailing list.

The mailing pack, i.e. what goes in the envelope, we shall look at later. As for the mailing list, i.e. who you send your envelopes to, it cannot be emphasised enough that getting the list right must be given top priority, for it is every bit as important (many would argue more important) as getting the enclosures right. What is the point in sending appeals for money to people who hardly have enough to live on themselves? Don't waste money asking people in the south of England to help a hostel in the north of Scotland; it will seem too remote to them and there are plenty of hostels on the doorstep needing help. They might support polar bears at the North Pole, though. The whole point about direct mail is that you can target. You can write to people with a proclivity to give to your cause, thus maximising your return. But how do you target? How do you get the right mailing list? Essentially you have three choices:

- you can rent a ready-made list

- you can have a list put together for you

- or you can compile your own list

Off-the-Peg Jobs

An off-the-peg list is a bit like a ready-to-wear suit; it will cost you less than its tailor-made equivalent, but the fit might not be quite so good. Mailing lists can be hired quite cheaply via list-brokers. A list broker will advise you on the sort of list that is most suitable for your needs, or which selections from within lists. Their advice is normally free – they earn their crust from commissions paid by list owners.

Generally you will hire a list, not buy it. In other words, you will be given a list and you will agree how many times you will use it. The hire price depends on this. The people on your list are known as 'cold prospects'. However, once they respond to your mailing, they become 'warm prospects'.

When you hire a mailing list, it will be classified. In other words, the list owner will compile it so that everyone on the list shares certain characteristics. These might be to do with income, lifestyle, attitudes and beliefs, or where they live – or a combination of these factors. For example:

- people who live in a particular area e.g. Birmingham or the West Midlands.
- or a particular type of area e.g. a high status retirement area with many single people.
- or in particular housing e.g. new council estates in inner cities.

As you can see, it is possible to be quite precise about the type of person you wish to mail to, although inevitably there will be some wastage in even the best mailing lists. There are a number of systems for classifying mailing lists; the two main ones are ACORN and MOSAIC (see Chapter Thirteen).

When hiring a mailing list, there are certain questions you should ask. These are:

- how was the list compiled? Where did the names come from?
- how has the list performed? What have response rates been for other users of this list?
- how up-to-date is the list? How often is it updated and when was the last update?
- what will the list cost? What do your get for your money e.g. how often can you use the list and over what period? Are there any additional costs?
- is the list registered under the Data Protection Act?
- has the list been cleaned against the Mailing Preference Service's list? (See below.)
- is the list available in the form that suits you best e.g. sticky labels, computer disk?
- is the list post coded, so you can sort it and qualify for Mailsort postage discounts? (See below.)

Tailor-Made For You

Clearly a tailor-made list is better, fitting much more closely with what you are looking for. A

> **TIP**
>
> *Don't waste money or spoil your reputation by writing to people who do not want unsolicited mail. Consumers who do not want 'junk' mail can register their details with the Mailing Preference Scheme (see address list), who produce regularly updated lists of everyone who has contacted them. The list can be bought for £100 plus VAT and used to 'clean' general lists. Hopefully this makes everyone happy: consumers do not get unwanted mail and organisations do not waste money writing to people who have no interest.*

tailor-made list will not be made from scratch: it will use parts of a list, perhaps merged with another mailing list, giving you the sort of coverage you require.

Home Made Lists

Many organisations believe that a home-made list is cheaper than an off-the-peg one, because you have not had to pay for it. But when you take staff costs into account, your own list could work out very expensive if you are constructing it from scratch. However, research has shown that the names and addresses of your existing 'customers' are, on average, three times as likely to respond to your mailings as 'cold prospects'.

The best home-made lists are those you already have, and if you are at all organised, you should have a database in any case. With personal computers now virtually universal, even in the smallest charities, there are few excuses for not compiling lists as part of your everyday work. (You can buy software to help you construct mailing lists and databases on your computer.) You might need to refine a list, and you must spend time keeping lists up to date, but hopefully you will already have the makings of a list. This might be made up of:

- people who have bought from you/donated to you in the past.

- people who currently give to you.

- people who have telephoned or written in for further information, both recently and in the past.

- people who are current members or subscribers.

- people who have entered any competitions you have run (this can be a good way of building up a list in-house).

You can also build lists using the local telephone directory, Yellow Pages and Thomson Directories (for business addresses), and the electoral register.

You may find that you need a number of different lists. Greenpeace group their members into several lists, so they know which members are interested in supporting campaigns, which are willing

TRUE STORY

A small charity launched a 'wills' campaign, in conjunction with a firm of solicitors. For a £25 donation to the charity, the law firm would draw up a will free of charge. With wills normally costing from £80-£100, this represented a good deal for those taking part. To minimise wastage and maximise return, the charity asked the firm to extract from its database those clients without a will. The charity then wrote to them, via the solicitors (to protect confidentiality), pointing out that they had no will, summarising the benefits of having a will (and the potential problems of not having one) and drawing their attention to the special offer. Take up was very high for a direct mail campaign, thanks to effective targeting. It took longer to produce the mailing list than it would have taken to write to all the firm's clients, but there was no wastage and the more tailored approach paid dividends.

TIP

Royal Mail offer a discount (of between 13% and 32%) for 4000+ letters of the same size and weight which you sort by postcode and bundle yourself. This is known as Mailsort. They also provide free collection for 1000 letters or more. They offer a range of other services which charities using direct mail could benefit from and should be contacted for further details of these.

to join local groups, and which are likely to buy from their mail order catalogue. How do they know all this? They ask. A welcome pack for new supporters asks them to tell Greenpeace what interests them. Greenpeace can then target mailings more accurately and avoid waste and unnecessary expense.

DATABASES: A GLORIFIED MAILING LIST?

It is important that you recognise the difference between a mailing list and a database. A mailing list is simply a list or lists of names and addresses. A database includes other details too, such as whether people have donated to you, when, how much, in what form and so on. It might have someone's sex, age, the number of times they have given, over what period etc. In other words, a database gives you a clearer picture, and enables you easily to extract particular groups. A good database would enable you to pull out all female donors over 60 who have donated £10 or more in the last six months, for example.

TIP

Don't put every scrap of information you have on your database. This will slow your computer and make information retrieval tedious and frustrating. Record only the information that will be of use to you. And as with mailing lists, keep it all up-to-date.

THE DATA PROTECTION ACT

There are various software packages on the market to help you establish databases and many computers now come with the software ready-installed. Remember, though, that you are required by law to register as a data user with the Data Protection Register. This is not complicated and a quick call to the DPR on 01625 535777 will provide you with all the information you need.

Having looked at the importance of getting the right list we now turn to the contents of your mailing. This will include:

TRUE STORY

I have found my way onto two different mailing lists, in one case as Ms A and in the second case as Mr Moy. Any mail arriving for me so addressed goes unopened into the bin. It is really important to get people's names right when you write to them. If you are hiring a mailing list, find out from the list broker or owner what steps they take to check their lists for accuracy.

■ the envelope you send the mailing in.

■ the covering letter.

■ any other enclosures.

Assuming that your mailing list is a good one, your mailing will reach people who are likely to regard your charity favourably. But that's only half the battle. The contents of your mailing need to persuade them to help, to join, to buy or to give. Successfully targeted mailings can be let down by a poorly produced package.

THE ENVELOPE

Let's start on the outside, with the envelope.

To Print Or Not To Print

You have two options when it comes to envelopes:

- you can used readily available stationers' envelopes, off-the-shelf, as it were.

- or you can have envelopes specially printed for you, with a design or message on the outside.

Many charities have envelopes printed specially for them, with messages urging the recipient to open the mailing. In 1995, when the Samaritans launched its 'One Number' campaign, to publicise that it now has one local number giving callers access to a network of over 200 branches, it used direct mail to help raise funds to support the new service. The envelopes were printed with the message: "Please open immediately – time sensitive material" and they brought in £58,000 in donations in just ten days. Some organisations use photographs to support the message, such as forlorn looking animals, deprived children or other images designed to elicit pity or sympathy (though many charities are wary of using exploitative or emotive imagery).

Charities which produce their own printed envelopes presumably do so because they believe that the cost of design and print are more than recouped by this approach. However, as the true story above shows, at least one charity has found that mailings that look like 'normal' letters elicit the best response for them. You need to decide what's best for you, to carefully weigh up the costs and benefits before making your decision, and ideally do a split test mailing to be sure you take the right decision.

> **TRUE STORY**
>
> *A charity carried out a 'split test' mailing to assess whether the appearance of direct mail has any effect on the response rates. Five types of envelopes were sent out. The one that looked most like a proper letter, with typed address and postage stamp, was found to be twice as effective as the one that looked most like 'junk' mail, even though the enclosures were identical.*

> **TIP**
>
> *One point to consider is that if you have specially printed envelopes, you will get a message across even if the envelope is never opened. I recently received a mailing from Oxfam, and printed on the envelope was the message "Over 90p in every £1 goes to fund our vital work on behalf of the poorest people of the world." This important message could influence the recipient at some later date, even if they fail to respond to this particular mailing. Having said that, it could be argued that a plain envelope has to be opened, if only to check what's inside. It is easier to bin mail if you know at a glance that it is unsolicited.*

Size is Important

Whether you choose ready made or specially printed envelopes, you need to decide on the size (which, of course, will be dependent on the size of the enclosures).

Royal Mail find it easier to process some envelopes than others, now that their sorting is automated.

> **TIP**
>
> *Use standard sized small envelopes (e.g. approx. 9"x4") as these tend to get opened first, for they most resemble 'normal' mail. Larger envelopes delivered to people's homes tend to get opened last, or not at all.*

They recommend that envelopes are:

- between 140mm and 240mm long.

- between 165mm and 90mm wide.

- oblong in shape.

- the longer side is at least 1.4 times the length of the shorter.

The common envelope sizes DL (to take one third A4) and C5 (to take half A4) fall into Royal Mail's preferred range. They cannot handle envelopes smaller than 100mmx70mm or larger than 610mmx460mm.

THE ENCLOSURES

Now to the enclosures. Remember that all advertising, even direct mail (postal advertising), should measure up to the AIDA yardstick (see Chapter Eight on advertising). Your mailing should attract attention, stimulate interest and desire, and prompt action.

TRUE STORY

I once received a letter in a plain white envelope. Across the envelope's opening, at the back, stamped in red ink, were the words "Opened for inspection." The envelope had indeed been opened, and resealed with sellotape. I was furious at this intrusion. On opening the letter myself, I discovered that it was an elaborate gimmick to attract my attention. The enclosure was a mailshot from The Observer newspaper. It began: "Imagine the outrage you'd feel if you discovered your mail had been tampered with." It was promoting a series of articles on censorship. It was gimmicky but highly effective.

Most mailings comprise a covering letter and one enclosure. The enclosure may be:

- a mail order catalogue.

- an order form.

- a membership leaflet.

- a questionnaire.

- a promotional or information leaflet.

- a newsletter.

- a pre-paid envelope.

TRUE STORY: GETTING IT RIGHT

The charity CBF World Jewish Relief sent vacuum sealed sandwiches to over 20,000 Jewish households in the London area. The packaging was printed with: "This sandwich can feed a family of 3 for a month". In place of a filling in the sandwich was a printed appeal setting out the desperate position of people in Belgrade and seeking money to send boxes of food to them. It was an unusual direct mailshot, specially designed to make people take notice and hopefully take action too.

Be careful not to include too many enclosures, as this will burden the recipient and swell your postage bill. Decide on the maximum weight of your mailing before it is produced, and make sure you do not exceed it to the extent that you are pushed into the next mailing band.

TRUE STORY: GETTING IT WRONG

Food was used in a mailshot to promote Scotland to travel writers. Across Britain freelance journalists specialising in travel were sent a small haggis as part of their mailshot. It certainly attracted attention, but for the wrong reasons. The package arrived at the height of the summer, when most recipients were away. In the heat, the haggis festered behind their front door, welcoming them back to bad food and a rotten smell! If you want to use a gimmick, that's fine. They can be very effective, but do think it through first.

The Covering Letter

Take time over the preparation of your covering letter. It is the thread that holds the whole mailing together, so get it right. This is more important still if your letter is the only enclosure. It must capture the recipient's interest very quickly, or it will never be read. You need to ensure that your covering letter is:

TIP

You should aim for your covering letter and contents to emerge from the envelope the right way up. Preferably the letter and enclosures should be folded in the same direction, to make opening the mailing that bit easier.

- **short:** preferably no more than one side. However, if you do go onto two sides, end page one with a split sentence to encourage the reader to turn the page.

- **personal:** so the recipient feels that a real, committed person has written it, and that the letter is appealing direct to them. Use the words 'you' and 'your'.

- **persuasive:** puts forward clear and strong arguments for why their help/action/ membership is necessary.

- **appropriate:** uses appropriate language to set the tone and appeal to the reader.

- **urges action:** by making the reader feel that they can do something to help.

TIP

Many organisations print a PS (post script) on the letter in a hand-written style, so that this stands out from the rest of the letter. It often says something like "Hurry – offer only available until" or "Remember that your help can make all the difference to children like ..." The aim is to ensure that even if recipients do not read all the letter, the PS will stand out enough for them to at least read that. It should have a tone of urgency, or should aim to encourage action.

Other Enclosures

Your covering letter should signpost readers to the enclosure(s). Both your covering letter and other enclosures should be attractively produced, although care should be taken to ensure that they do not appear expensive or wasteful. This would clearly be counter-productive.

You should not only keep enclosures to a minimum, you should keep each one as short as it can be. All of us suffer from information overload and there are limits to what we can absorb. Added to that, the increasing pressures on our time, combined with the explosion in direct mail, mean that we have more to deal with than we can manage. Don't add to the burden by sending out jumbo-sized mailings.

Bear in mind that your enclosures need not be written material. Companies, and some charities, now mail videos in place of leaflets and brochures. The RSPCA has been using video for a number of years, targeting high-value donors. Its videos explain how the charity's money is being spent, and appeal for donations. The RSPCA says that the response it gets from video is twice as high as for a standard letter mailing. The average donation is also significantly higher. Of course you need to remember that producing a video is more expensive, and packaging and mailing costs are also greater. But for some charities, such as the RSPCA, this is a worthwhile investment.

> **TIP**
>
> *Your direct mail letter and other enclosures should be designed to reinforce your corporate identity. In other words, make good use of your logo, print in your house colours etc. so recipients can see at a glance who their mailing is from.*

Seven Golden Rules for Effective Fundraising Direct Mail Campaigns

1. Write in plain English explaining what a difference the reader's help can make.

2. Keep the covering letter short and to the point.

3. Don't exaggerate how much you need or how serious the problem is.

4. Use emotion if appropriate.

5. Use case histories if appropriate (anonomysing them if necessary, to ensure confidentiality).

6. Make it easy for recipients to respond/take action.

7. Make the mailing look attractive – but not lavish.

MAKING IT EASY TO RESPOND

Sometimes direct mail is used merely to inform. Generally, however, it is intended to fundraise or to encourage recipients to take action of some sort. It is in your interests to consider how you can make it easy for them to act. Your success depends on the ease with which you enable people to do something.

You need to use a combination from the list below to ensure that action can be taken with ease:

■ **Response device**
   If you want people to order from you, to send a donation or to join your organisation, you need to make it really easy. They are less likely to write you a letter than to complete a simple tear-off slip or coupon. Remember this when designing your mailing. Include a membership form, a banker's order form, or another device to allow easy response.

■ **Business Reply**
   This is one of Royal Mail's response services, which have been designed to encourage customers to respond by enabling you

to pay their postage. Research by the Direct Mail Information Service in 1993 showed that paying the postage for your customer's reply will increase response. Envelopes or cards pre-printed with your address make it really easy for recipients of your mail to respond. If you think this is likely to increase take-up for you, and that the long-term benefits will outweigh the cost involved, why not try it out?

■ Freepost

This is another Royal Mail response service. Your enquirers or donors can write to you post-free, though you will have to pick up the tab. It will cost you the postage charge, plus an annual licence fee, plus a small handling charge per item. Talk to the local Royal Mail Sales Centre by calling 0345 950 950. All calls are charged at local rates.

■ Freephone

Both British Telecom and Mercury offer Freephone numbers, which work in a similar way to Freepost. Call them for details. Remember that to the cost of such services you need to add the cost of staffing telephone lines to handle responses. Research has shown that people generally prefer to respond by post rather than by telephone.

> **TRUE STORY**
>
> *Some charities aim for the best of both worlds: they use a Freepost address, but encourage respondents to use a stamp when replying. Oxfam, for example, includes in its direct mail a pre-printed envelope which says: "No stamp needed, but using one will save Oxfam money". Marie Curie Cancer Care carries a slightly longer message expressing the same sentiment: "No stamp is needed – but if you kindly use a stamp more of your gift will go to caring for people with cancer. Thank you."*

■ Credit card payment

By offering the facility of paying or donating by credit card, you make it even easier for people to respond. A Freephone credit card hotline makes it easier still. Remember that the costs to you will include the 'merchant fee' charged by the credit card company, which will be a percentage of each credit card transaction. Weigh up carefully whether credit cards are right for your organisation, by working out the costs and the benefits.

COPING WITH THE RESPONSE

You undertake direct mail campaigns with the expectation that they will be successful – you want people to respond, and respond in numbers. But are you geared up to cope with the response? Do you have enough staff available to process donations/activate new memberships/send out information packs? When undertaking a direct mail campaign:

> **TIP**
>
> *You can encourage response to your mailing by including a 'speed incentive'. For example, your mailing could say "Reply before July 1st and get a free 'Save the Dolphin' lapel badge".*

Some Do's and Don'ts

✔ **do** tell everyone who needs to know and brief staff who answer the phone.

✗ **don't** do it so it coincides with a really busy period in your organisation, such as your Christmas newsletter mailing.

✔ **do** have enough people to answer the phone (your mailing may generate extra calls) and to deal with responses.

✗ **don't** leave it all to the last minute. Plan your response before your mailing takes place; leave it 'til afterwards and you're in trouble.

THE HIDDEN COSTS OF DIRECT MAIL

It is easy to think that the only costs involved in direct mail are postage charges. Here are some others you will need to budget for:

■ **the mailing list** – hiring one or building your own.

■ **envelopes** – buying them from wholesalers or having your own designed and printed.

■ **design** – the cost of having envelopes, covering letters and enclosures (such as leaflets) designed.

■ **printing** – the cost of having the above items printed, including the cost of paper.

■ **copywriting** – if you want your enclosures professionally written, you will need to budget for this.

■ **photography** – if you are producing special enclosures, you may need to commission photography.

■ **response device** – if you are planning to use a Freepost address or other response device to encourage recipients to reply, you will need to add the cost of this to your overall budget.

■ **stuffing envelopes** – the time involved in stuffing, sealing and sorting envelopes is immense and you will need to budget for this. There are companies who will do it for you – mailing houses – or you can do it in-house, possibly using volunteers. However, do not underestimate the time and effort (and boredom!) involved.

■ **project management** – whether you co-ordinate all of the above in-house, or use a specialist direct marketing agency to oversee it for you, it will cost.

■ **follow-up** – processing responses to direct mail takes time and costs money (though it hopefully generates money too!).

■ **evaluation** – you should always spend time afterwards analysing the success of a direct mail campaign (see below).

> **TIP**
> If using a designer, copywriter or agency to produce your mailing, give them a comprehensive written brief. This will make their job easier and you will get a more suitable and effective end result.

USING THE INTERNET FOR DIRECT MAIL

A small number of charities – Greenpeace, Friends of the Earth and Comic Relief included – are hopeful that the Internet will prove an effective vehicle for fundraising and attracting new members. The charity Heartwise promoted itself on the World Wide Web and attracted 200 new members in one month. Those giving or joining via the Internet can then be direct-mailed using E-mail. The benefit is that mailshots can be sent from one end of the country to the other, or even across the globe, for the price of a local phone call. If you are on the Internet, think about whether you can get it to work for you.

EVALUATION

As with most aspects of marketing, evaluation should be an integral part of the process. You need to measure the cost and effectiveness of direct mail campaigns in the same way as you would measure the success of a press advertising campaign.

There are two standard measures which are used to measure the effectiveness of mailings:

1. **cost per response:** add together all the costs associated with your direct mail campaign. Now divide by the number of responses received.

2. **cost per conversion:** here you divide the cost of the mailing by the number of 'sales' – or donations, memberships, subscriptions.

As you can see, the cost per response will inevitably be lower than the cost per conversion. You need to work out in advance how much you can afford to spend on each sale. There's no simple answer for this; it all depends on how much a customer is worth. If you have to spend £25 to get one customer, but each customer will donate around £2,000 to you in their lifetime, and one in ten customers will also leave you a legacy, £25 is a small price to pay.

Based on your allowable cost per conversion, you need to set targets right at the outset. As part of your evaluation you should review these targets. Assuming your allowable cost per conversion is £50 and your mailing list is 1,000 people, you will need to receive 20 sales (assuming each mailing costs £1) for you to cover costs. More than 20 sales and you are beginning to see a return on your direct mail investment.

The Post Mortem

Part of your evaluation should also include a post mortem to see what lessons you can learn to help improve future mailings. The sample post mortem checklist on the next page will help you to see some of the factors that you may wish to consider when reviewing the success of a campaign.

> **TIP**
> *Royal Mail produce an excellent Direct Mail Guide, full of tips and advice on direct mail. The guide also includes examples of charity direct mail, including mailings by the Salvation Army and Marie Curie Cancer Care. It is available free from Royal Mail Customer Sales Centres (see address list).*

Sample direct mail post mortem

Campaign name:

Mailing date:	Quantity mailed:

Number of 'gone-aways' returned: Number of donations received on first mail-out:

Number of enquiries for more information: Number of these which then sent in donation:

Total cost of mailings (inc. inserts and staff time): £

Cost of sending out additional information: £

Total donations received: £   Cost of mailing per donation: £

Average donation size: £

%age of recipients sending in donation (total)

%age of recipients sending in donation (after first mailing)

%age of mailing sending in donation (after requesting further information)

How could the mailing package be improved?

■ letter design: ■ letter content:

■ enclosed leaflet design: ■ leaflet content:

■ envelope design: ■ other:

How did the various suppliers perform? Any comments?

■ designer: ■ copywriter:

■ printer: ■ stationer:

■ list broker: ■ Royal Mail:

■ others:

Where could savings be made?

Were there any additional costs we had not anticipated?

How did we handle responses in-house? Could we have done better? How?

Overall how could the campaign's success be rated? Did it meet its objectives?

What are the recommendations for future mailings?

DIRECT ADVERTISING

Be careful not to confuse direct mail and direct advertising. Direct mail is just that, mail which goes direct to a household. By contrast direct advertising is not mailed, it is dropped through people's letterboxes, often though not necessarily in a free newspaper, and is usually in the form of a leaflet without an envelope.

Direct advertising has many advantages for charities:

- it is cheap (especially if you can find volunteers to do the mail-drop).

- it can be used by very small charities.

- it is especially effective for local groups.

- it can be targeted at particular types of neighbourhood.

Royal Mail offer a **Door to Door** service which enables you to deliver promotional material nationwide (or just in one or two areas, depending on your needs), reaching recipients at the same time as their regular post. The cost depends on the volume and weight of the items you are sending, but works out very reasonable. I received a mailing from Oxfam this way, which had in the place of the postmark a message saying: "Delivered by hand to save money".

HAVE A GO YOURSELF

The following is a direct mail letter written to someone you have not had contact with before. You know that the recipient is female, middle-aged and has a family.

THE ACTION TRUST FOR THE PREVENTION OF SUDDEN INFANT DEATH SYNDROME

City Scope House, 2nd Floor, 22 Buccleuch Street, Easingswold ES10 42P

Tel. 014452 332267 Fax 014452 332268

Philip Davies OBE, Honourable Secretary

Dear Mrs Smith,

The Action Trust for the Prevention of Sudden Infant Death Syndrome is a national charity registered with the Charity Commission. Established since 1987, we have invested heavily in research using the top experts in this field – consultant paediatricians, pathologists, leading scientists and others – to help uncover the causes of sudden infant death syndrome (SIDS). We hope that our extensive and exhaustive SIDS research programme will be successful in identifying the causes of sudden infant death syndrome. This will enable us to draw up an action programme aimed at eradicating SIDS once and for all.

You can help us by funding our vital research. We need to fund a research worker, which will cost us £25,000 plus national insurance, car, expenses and other overheads. All of this will come to £40,000 for one researcher for one year. Since we need to fund the post for two years, we need £80,000. Please help us by sending in a donation. Make your cheque payable to The Action Trust for the Prevention of Sudden Infant Death Syndrome and send it to Philip Davies OBE, Honourable Secretary, The Action Trust for the Prevention of Sudden Infant Death Syndrome, City Scope House, 2nd Floor, 22 Buccleuch Street, Easingswold ES10 42P.

Thank you for reading this letter. We are sure that you will not let us down in our vital research and look forward to receiving your cheque.

Yours sincerely

Philip Davies OBE
Honourable Secretary

What's Wrong With It?

If that letter landed on my door mat, along with the rest of my mail, I'm afraid it would rapidly become a resident of the waste paper basket. What was wrong with it?

- SIDS is the correct name, but we all talk about cot death. If your charity uses jargon, try to speak to ordinary donors in plain English.

- the letter fails to engage the reader right at the outset.

- it reads in an impersonal way.

- there is no emotion, no compassion and no appeal to the heartstrings.

- the charity needs £80,000. It might be legitimate expenditure, but the way it is presented, it doesn't sound like it.

- there is no indication of what size of donation is acceptable – 50p? £10?

- the address is too long and does not need to be repeated in the body copy as it already appears on the letterhead.

- it is a bit presumptive to assume that people *will* give! Don't use sentences like: "We are sure that you will not let us down in our vital research and look forward to receiving your cheque."

This version is far better:

THE ACTION TRUST FOR THE PREVENTION OF SUDDEN INFANT DEATH SYNDROME

City Scope House, 2nd Floor, 22 Buccleuch Street, Easingswold ES10 42P

Tel. 014452 332267 Fax 014452 332268

Philip Davies OBE, Honourable Secretary

Dear Mrs Smith,

You are a mother, so you'll understand how we feel. Our son, Jason, was born a beautiful, happy, healthy baby. You can imagine our relief. We were the proud parents of a strong and lively boy. But our joy soon turned to despair, for our lovely son died suddenly just a few weeks later. It is hard to believe that the child I carried inside me for nine months is now dead. Jason would have been celebrating his second birthday soon. Instead of having a party for him we will be visiting his grave. The pain will always be with us, and nothing can remove our loss, but you can help to ensure that your own grandchildren do not face Jason's fate. Support The Action Trust for the Prevention of Sudden Infant Death Syndrome and help make cot death a thing of the past.

Jason died suddenly and no one knows why. We didn't even get a chance to say good-bye or to prepare ourselves for the pain. Thousands of parents across Britain know our heartache because they too have lost their babies in this way. The only good thing to come out of our own loss is the establishment of this charity, which will help ensure that other babies like Jason do not have to die so needlessly.

For just 30p per day you can fund our vital research programme, which aims to uncover the reasons for cot death. Though it is still a mystery to scientists the world over, our own research staff have made several important breakthroughs which have brought us all closer to knowing why babies like Jason die. If you can afford to help us, please send a cheque today (made payable to The Action Trust for the Prevention of Sudden Infant Death Syndrome). Donations large and small are very welcome.

Yours sincerely

Jenny Estelle – Jason's mum

Discussion

What makes this second letter so much better?

- ■ it is written by someone who has lost a child through cot death, so it is more heart-felt than a letter from a remote honoourable secretary.

- ■ it aims to stir the emotions and prompt action.

- ■ its use of the experience of a real mother talking about her real baby makes it all the more real. Reading about second-hand experiences is never quite the same.

- ■ it is one mother talking to another mother.

- ■ it engages the reader by asking her to put herself in the writer's shoes.

- ■ it refers to SIDS by its popular name, cot death.

- ■ it quantifies what helping means – just 30p a day.

CHAPTER ELEVEN

PROMOTION – OTHER METHODS

What's in this chapter?

■ *an A to Z of promotional opportunities.*

■ *using bus and bus ticket advertising.*

■ *tapping the potential of promotional leaflets, newsletters and magazines.*

■ *exploiting the promotional potential of annual reports and other publications.*

■ *using exhibitions and roadshows.*

■ *open days, talks and seminars.*

■ *sponsorship – giving it and getting it.*

■ *choosing the right promotional vehicle.*

Preceding chapters have covered media advertising, editorial and direct mail. These are by no means the only promotional vehicles available to you. There are all sorts of other ways of promoting your products, services and events. Many can be done in-house at little or no cost, while others will require significant expenditure.

AN A TO Z OF PROMOTIONAL OPPORTUNITIES

A

Answering machines – you can use your office answer machine message as an advertising opportunity by recording details of how people can help the cause or make a donation.

Audio cassettes – many people drive to work and 90% of motorists have cassette players in their car. Audio tapes can be a good way of reaching people with your promotional message. Tapes can be cost effective, and they can even be done in-house. Because they have a higher perceived value than a newsletter or leaflet, as well as novelty value, they are perhaps less likely to be binned.

B

Bins – some companies sponsor litterbins in town centres and there could be scope for certain charities doing this as an appropriate way of promoting a message.

Bags – plastic carrier bags with your logo and message printed on them can make useful give-aways.

C

Cinema – cinema advertising is a particularly good way of reaching the 15-24-year-old age-group. The benefits are that it is cheaper than TV advertising, you show to a captive audience and the screen size offers maximum impact for your commercial. On the downside it can be expensive to make the commercials, and there is the added expense of having to pay for the 'airtime'. You would probably need to buy in external help.

Collection sacks – if you drop collection sacks through doors, to collect unwanted goods for resale in charity shops etc., use the bag containing the sack to promote your message. Shelter carry the following message on their bags: "Shelter gives advice and hope to the homeless. Why not volunteer in one of our shops and help us raise funds. Your nearest Shelter shop is …".

D

Directories – carefully placed adverts in relevant directories and handbooks can be effective, but only if the readers form part of your target audience. Some charities advertise in legal handbooks to ensure that their charity is known to lawyers, who may be asked for advice on which charities to leave a legacy to.

E

Eggs – messages can be blown with high pressure jets onto the outside of fresh eggs. They offer scope for highly original and creative advertising.

E-mail – to send E-mail you need a modem (which can be bought for less than £100), a computer and a subscription to a service-provider such as CompuServe (less than £10 per month). You can then send messages electronically in seconds anywhere in the world for the price of a local phone call. As more people get 'online', more charities will make use of E-mail as a cost-effective promotional tool.

F

Flags – a number of companies specialise in flag-making (see the Yellow Pages for a company near you). They are surprisingly good value for money and offer a novel way of promoting your message.

G

Give-aways – cheap free promotional items such as balloons or biros can carry your advertising, educational or health promotion message.

H

Hoardings – Hoardings form part of a type of advertising known as 'outdoor'. They (and other forms of outdoor advertising) are now widely used by the larger charities. Research shows that two weeks is the optimum time for a hoarding advert to be displayed; awareness peaks on the tenth day and then declines. Each poster site has an OSCAR (Outdoor Site Classification and Audience Research) which is an individual score based on traffic flow past the site, position of the board and so on. An OSCAR of 89 (about average) means that the poster is passed by around 89,000 people each week. Motorists seeing your poster have around seven seconds to take it in, so it must be big, bold and very simple.

I

Inserts – inserted leaflets in magazines and journals are a cheaper method of distribution than direct mail.

Internet – the growth in popularity of the Internet offers opportunities for promoting your work and your services. Amnesty International, for example, gets 1,500 visitors a day to its 'World-Wide Web page' and uses electronic mail to update members. You don't need to be a big charity to make effective use of the Internet. It can even be used to sell products. High Street names such as Virgin Megastores, Dixons, Tesco, Selfridges and WH Smith are among the many companies now offering 'online' shopping. If you sell by mail order, why not investigate the Internet?

J

Junk mail – this is the derogatory term for direct mail, which is covered in Chapter Ten.

K

Key rings – many charities produce key rings with their logo or promotional message. They are cheap to produce, can be sold to recoup the cost, and have a long 'shelf-life'.

L

LED displays – some public places such as swimming pools and sports centres offer an advertising service via large LED displays which display your message. It is a cheap and easy way to advertise.

M

Meeting rooms – Your meeting rooms should display your promotional material so that visitors can see it and be influenced by it. So should your reception.

N

Newsletters – your newsletter should be seen as a promotional as well as an information vehicle (see below).

O

Outlets – use other organisations' outlets (shops, offices, drop-in centres etc.) as opportunities to promote yourself, via exhibitions/displays, or by leaving posters and leaflets.

P

Pay and display car parking tickets – in many towns and cities it is possible to advertise on the back of these.

Posters – whether you get them properly printed or make your own, you can reach a lot of people with a poster.

Postcards – most trendy cafés and restaurants in our major towns now have free postcard dispensers. Customers can pick up attractive and free postcards, while advertisers can benefit from a new advertising option that is also cost-effective. During France's nuclear tests in the Pacific in 1995, one pressure group produced a postcard showing a nuclear explosion. On the reverse was the message "Stop the nuclear tests now" and the card was addressed to Jacques Chirac, French President. This was a clever way of getting an important message across to the British public and providing them with an easy way to take action and register their displeasure, while simultaneously showing the French government the strength of international feeling about nuclear tests.

Post Office franks – if you don't have your own franking machine, you can still get your message across by getting the post office to frank other people's letters with your logo.

Programmes – when exhibiting at a conference you can often place an advert in the conference programme. Other types of programme are often also available for charity advertising, such as theatre programmes, for example. They can be effective in reaching decision-makers and wealthy donors

Q

Questionnaires – you should not conduct a questionnaire survey merely as a way of promoting your organisation, but do remember that it can serve the dual purpose of gaining you useful information while at the same time helping you promote your name and your aims.

R

Railways – many different advertising opportunities are offered at railways and on Railtrack land. Collectively this form of advertising is known as 'transport advertising' (see below).

S

Sandwich boards – these have novelty value and are a cheap way of promoting an event – providing you can find enough amenable volunteers to pound the pavements!

Stickers – once stuck down, stickers have great staying power and so you message remains on view for a long time, thus increasing the number of opportunities for it to be seen and read.

Stationery – your own letterhead, compliments slips and other stationery offer a good opportunity to promote an important message. If your organisation does not have a strapline (a short and snappy statement of purpose – Shelter's is: The Campaign For Homeless People) why not devise one and use it on your stationery to explain your work or promote a cause?

T

Taxis – taxi cabs can display adverts, both inside and outside the cabs. Some are also fitted with leaflet dispensers.

Transport advertising – this covers everything from adverts inside and outside buses (see separate section below) to posters on the London Underground, in lifts, escalators, and trains. The benefit of this method is that you are reaching an audience which is bored, often stationary, and in need of something to divert them. Transport advertising can therefore be very effective.

U

Umbrellas – golfing umbrellas were once synonymous with corporate entertainment, but many charities have since started to produce promotional items of this sort. Unlike those produced by companies, charity umbrellas are usually produced for sale, not as give-aways.

V

Vehicles – you can use your own cars and minibuses as mobile adverts, as well as buses, trains and tubes.

Video – although expensive, video can be a powerful way of getting your message across in a highly visual and digestible way.

Visors – visors, baseball caps and other promotional clothing items are available from many different companies at quite reasonable prices. They can be personalised with your logo and message.

W

Windows – many charities work from shopfront premises; learn a trick from the big department stores and arrange attractive promotional displays aimed at stopping passers-by in their tracks and getting them to peek in. Note that you will need more than a collection of yellowed press cuttings, dog-eared publications and decomposing dead bluebottles to achieve this.

X

Xtra curricula work – remember that your own staff can be your best advertisements. What they say about your organisation 'after hours' will have a significant bearing on your reputation.

Y

Yellow Pages – most charities have an entry in Yellow Pages. If you plan to have more than just a lineage advert, think carefully about the design and wording of your advert; after all, if you are going to the expense of paying for an advert, you should take care to maximise your return.

Year Planners – a number of voluntary organisations produce year planners. The benefit is that they remain in use and on display for a whole year, making them very effective. However, they will only be put on display if they are attractively produced.

Z

Zany gimmicks – by using your imagination, you can come up with unusual gimmicks that help you promote an important message. When British Telecom cut the price of calls to America, it needed to publicise this to its target audience. As New York is known as the Big Apple, apples were used as the promotional vehicle. The price cut message was printed on small fruit labels, which were then stuck to apples. The apples were handed out to transatlantic travellers arriving at Heathrow. Baskets of apples were also delivered to leading US companies with offices in London. A photocall was staged to secure media coverage too. It was a very cost-effective and imaginative way of promoting a message.

> **TIP**
>
> *Never overlook the obvious when it comes to promotion. A sign outside your office is a cheap and effective way of promoting yourself, particularly if you are on a busy street. Remember to check about planning permission.*

BUS ADVERTISING

Bus advertising is probably the only form of high profile advertising that is easily affordable for even the very smallest charities. You can advertise inside the bus and on the exterior. You can opt for a small panel on the back of the bus, or side panels in a variety of configurations. It works like this:

- look up 'advertising' in the Yellow Pages and find a company offering bus advertising (it should be clear from their advert or their name whether they offer this service).

- arrange for their sales representative to visit you

- their rep. will explain what bus advertising can do for you and will give you a rate card (this will set out what the cost is per panel per month for the various types of advertising panel).

- if you want to go ahead, the company will give you advice on your copy, will get artwork produced for you, and will arrange for your adverts to be printed (you can arrange this yourself, but it can be as cheap – and less hassle – to buy a whole package).

You can specify the type of bus you want your advert on (e.g. a double decker, a single decker etc.); you can say which depot(s) you want your bus(es) to run from; and you can specify towns and cities for your campaign. However, you cannot select particular routes. You can run a very local campaign (e.g. in just one town, or one part of a city) or you can go national (or any combination in between). This makes bus advertising very flexible, and as good for big charities as for small community groups.

> **TIP**
>
> *If you are advertising on a rear panel, your advert will be read by motorists and pedestrians on the move. That's why you must keep it short. If you say who you are, where you are and what you do, that's plenty.*

The Cost

An advert inside a bus can be as little as £10 per month, and it is often possible for a charity to get a discount on published rates. However, you need to add to this the cost of producing artwork (around £50) and the cost of production of your panels. A rear of bus advert (sized 20" by 48") would cost around £65 per panel per month.

Inside or Out?

Advertising inside a bus is cheaper than placing an ad on the exterior. You need to decide not only what your budget is, but who your target audience is, before you decide which to opt for. Those reading your advert on a bus may be very different to the sort of people who drive along behind buses. But there's another issue. What is your message? External advertising has to be short and sweet, given that you are displaying on a moving vehicle to people who are themselves on the move. Internal advertising, on the other hand, can be more expansive; it will be read by people with time to kill – people sitting on buses.

> **TRUE STORY**
>
> *A charity promoting a free and confidential counselling service for teenagers opted to advertise on the near side of the bus – the side that is seen when the bus is pulling into a bus stop. Why? Because its target audience – teenagers with problems – were those who spent their time hanging round bus shelters. Bus advertising was a cheap and effective way of promoting a service in a targeted way.*

BUS TICKET PROMOTIONS

Bus ticket advertising is cheaper than many other forms of promotion and can be effective, depending on who you are trying to reach. Obviously only bus passengers get to see your advertising, but if this is your target market, why not consider it? Given that tickets must be retained for the duration of a bus journey, passengers have ample time to look at your advert. Big brand names like Levi jeans use this medium. So do smaller organisations and public sector bodies.

Tickets are produced in full colour, for maximum impact. Image Promotions, which specialises in bus ticket advertising (see Chapter Fourteen), can help you plan a campaign, whether in just one town or a much wider area. They will make the booking with the bus company, do your artwork, printing, delivery and campaign monitoring. A full campaign starts from £450.

Who Travels by Bus?

Image Promotions, the company responsible for over 95% of all bus ticket promotions in the UK, provides the following figures for what it terms 'typical bus users':

Socio-economic group		Age group	
A	3%	15-19	9%
B	17%	20-34	22%
C1	26%	35-44	16%
C2	25%	45-54	14%
D	18%	55-64	12%
E	11%	65 and over	20%

Reasons for bus use			
Shops	56%	Work	18%
Social	12%	School	14%

> **TIP**
>
> *Use your fax header sheet as a promotional tool. The Directory of Social Change, publishers of this book, use theirs to carry details of forthcoming books. It costs them nothing extra but potentially increases their income from book sales. Think what you could promote with a short and simple message added to your fax header sheet.*

PROMOTIONAL LEAFLETS

Few organisations are without a promotional leaflet of some sort. For such an important document, the promotional leaflet is frequently given inadequate attention during its preparation. Remember that your leaflets are all-important; they are often the only contact people will have with your charity, so they must be professional and appealing. That's not to say that they must be glossy, simply that they should be well written, carefully thought through, and presented in a way that makes them easy to read and attractive to look at. Chances are that producing such a leaflet will involve investment, both of time and money. But the point about an investment is that there is a pay-off in the end, and that's what you are aiming for. By spending on a good and effective leaflet, you hope to improve your chances of donors giving, or individuals using your service, or people joining your campaign.

FIVE TIPS FOR BETTER LEAFLETS

1. plan the leaflet before you write it and establish the aim; is it to persuade, to educate, to inform?

2. use clear, plain language.

3. make it eye-catching, so people will want to look at it and read it.

4. don't try to put too much in; aim for two or three clear messages.

5. Remember to break up the text and to use illustrations where appropriate.

NEWSLETTERS AND MAGAZINES

Most charities and voluntary organisations produce newsletters, but many fail to see the role of these as marketing tools. Newsletters should not just be about news, they should also be regarded as opportunities to 'sell' a particular message, to ask for help or donations, to reach out to a particular group with a plea, and to present your image. A campaigning charity might wish to use its newsletter to encourage supporters to keep up their support and perhaps even extend it, to encourage new members to get involved, to inform so that supporters are knowledgeable about the issue, and perhaps even to ask for campaign funds. Naturally there would also be news in the form of campaign progress, updates and achievements.

> **TIP**
> *If you can only afford to print your newsletter in one colour, it is usually best to opt for black print on white paper, as everyone is used to this combination from reading newspapers and books. It is also a good combination for readers who have a slight visual impairment, as it provides a clear colour contrast.*

A fundraising charity might use its newsletter to showcase innovative fundraising initiatives, to suggest ideas for raising money, to thank those who have given, to show how the money has been spent, and to outline the continuing need for more money.

So remember, use your newsletters to promote your new products and services, to raise funds and awareness, and to attract and maintain support.

Five Tips for Better Newsletters

1. Make your cover page really attractive, to encourage readers to pick up the newsletter and delve inside.

2. Include a list of contents on the front page, again to entice readers inside.

3. Have regular features, such as 'Focus on Fundraising', 'Campaign Update', 'Members' News' etc. This will give your newsletter a familiar feel, which busy readers will appreciate.

4. Edit contributions; most will benefit from it.

5. Use articles of different lengths and remember to include lots of snippets.

OTHER PUBLICATIONS

Leaflets and newsletters are the main publications produced by charities. Most also produce an annual report, brochures and other reports, and posters. We cannot look here at all of the promotional literature charities produce, though we can focus on the main ones.

Indeed many of the rules will apply to all literature.

Annual Reports

Although charity annual reports are getting better, many charities regard their annual report as a yearly chore rather than a first rate opportunity to promote their organisation and its good work. Reports that are presented in a pedestrian fashion, with a series of statements by the Chair, Chief Executive etc. will fail to make a promotional impact. Indeed they may even damage the otherwise good promotional work you have achieved.

Annual reports are, of course, a review of the year, but that does not mean that you cannot also use them to promote the organisation as a whole, your approach and philosophy, your aims and objectives. You can use your report to explore or discuss important issues that relate to your work, and you can look to the future and flag up important events or new services planned for the coming years.

Five Tips for Better Annual Reports

1. Look at other charities' reports and copy their ideas, suitably adapted.

2. Ditch reports by the Chair, Director etc. and aim for a more imaginative approach. Perhaps try to write your report around a theme.

3. Try to avoid lists (e.g. a list of your staff, your supporters, your bankers and professional suppliers etc.) for they are a waste of valuable space.

4. Remember to use the back page.

5. Present your financial information in a lively way, so that even innumerate people like me can understand it! Remember that you do not have to reproduce your full accounts in your annual report; a summary is quite adequate. You must make full audited accounts available to anyone requesting them, but this need not be through your report.

TIP

If you are a fundraising charity, print on the back of your annual report an appeal for money or help. Or include a response form as an insert in the report.

Reports

When charities publish reports, they are usually on serious subjects. That does not mean that they need to be presented in a dull way or written in impenetrable language. Make reports readable and use them to market your organisation and its beliefs. A report is a 'selling' document; it should 'sell' its findings in order to promote a cause, attract funding, generate interest or whatever.

EXHIBITIONS

There are many opportunities for charities to exhibit in order to promote themselves or an aspect of their work. We will look at some of them below. But first, here are the three main types of exhibitions you may want to use:

1. Mobile Exhibitions

These should not be confused with portable exhibitions (see below). A mobile exhibition is one that you take out on the road, perhaps incorporated into a special caravan. Visitors enter your van or caravan to view your exhibition. It sounds an expensive production and it is. Not surprisingly, therefore, this method of exhibiting is used mainly by commercial organisations. However, there are many cases of charities and public sector organisations using mobile exhibitions to promote their service or message. Here are just three:

- the National Blood Transfusion Service is a good example that you may be familiar with. Their mobile Blood Donor van visits workplaces and shopping centres to promote blood donating, and it can even take people's blood there and then.

- an NHS trust uses a converted caravan to tour schools and nurseries delivering its oral hygiene message to children. The caravan is called the Dental Dream Machine, it is decorated with bright colours and cartoon characters, and aims to take the fear out of a trip to the dentist. Children go inside the caravan, view the equipment, ask the dentist questions, meet 'Denny the Dentosaurus' and pick up information leaflets.

- Greenpeace were concerned that half of all damaging fluorocarbons were leaked by supermarket freezers, in spite of alternative 'planet-friendly' freezers being available. All supermarket chains were receptive to Greenpeace's ideas on reducing damaging fluorocarbons, except Tesco. So in 1994, Greenpeace transformed a 40-foot articulated lorry into a mobile supermarket. It was fitted out with special 'Greenfreeze' freezers and painted to look like a Tesco lorry, but with the word 'Fiasco' instead of Tesco. Staff at Tesco's headquarters were invited inside and given leaflets. The lorry then toured Tesco stores across the UK. This was a huge mobile exhibition campaign with a difference, and done very cost-effectively. Nevertheless, it cost around £20,000, not counting staff time.

2. Portable Exhibitions

As the Greenpeace example shows, mobile exhibitions, while sometimes very effective, can also be very expensive. More within the means of the average charity is the portable exhibition. This comprises portable exhibition display boards, plus specially produced display material for attaching to the boards. Even this option is not cheap, with a display system costing anything from hundreds to thousands of pounds. Added to this is the cost of professionally producing material to display on the boards. (It can be done in-house – although generally not to the same standard.)

The advantage of a portable exhibition is that you can lend it to other organisations, to libraries, community centres etc. It therefore makes it a very easy way for you to promote your message. You can also easily take a portable exhibition with you when you attend talks and meetings.

3. Permanent Static Exhibitions

These are, obviously, exhibitions that stay put. Often they are too heavy to move and were designed for a particular place anyway. Many charity head offices have permanent exhibitions of their work.

Exhibit where?

You can exhibit:

- at other organisations' premises.
- at your own premises.
- at conferences, meetings and talks.
- outdoors – for example, in the High Street during a flag day, or at a sports event.

Five Reasons for Exhibiting

1. Staffed exhibition stands offer you a face-to-face opportunity to convert interested people, to get them to become members or to make a donation.

2. You can make new contacts which can be followed up later.

3. Exhibiting is a good opportunity for two-way communication. You can tell the punters about your charity, and also pick up views, opinions and feedback from them. Make sure you feed it all back to your organisation and take appropriate action.

4. You can use an exhibition to raise your profile.

5. Used carefully, exhibitions can be a cost-effective way of getting your message across.

Five tips for successful exhibitions

1. Free coffee at your exhibition stand can be a way of attracting people to it.

2. Have pens and paper to take details of people who want further information.

3. Make your exhibition as appealing as possible using flowers, seating, music, etc. as appropriate.

4. If your exhibition is staffed, ensure staff don't look as if they will pounce on anyone stopping to take a look – they should appear friendly and welcoming, but not pushy or suffocating.

5. Have a supply of promotional material available for visitors to take away.

OPEN DAYS

So many organisations hold open days, and so many of these events are a great flop. Having said that, they can also be an effective way of promoting your organisation or its services, if used with consideration. I have attended charity open days where staff outnumber visitors and there is apparently nothing to see. At such occasions, visitors shuffle about nervously, politely excuse themselves, and rush away vowing never to return. If that's what happens at your open days, you are defeating the object and damaging your reputation. Successful open days must:

- offer something to visitors to make their attendance worthwhile.

- attract the right target audience.

- have an appropriate staff/visitor ratio.

- follow-up new contacts after the event.

You need to be clear on why you are having an open day, what you want to achieve, who you want to attend, what you want them to go away with (information, for example, or a better understanding of your work). If you do all this, and you plan and promote your open day very carefully, you can have a very successful promotional event on your hands.

ROADSHOWS

Many charities now have roadshows, where they go on the road with their promotional message. It is not a cheap or easy way to promote your message, but it can be effective, provided:

- you cost the whole exercise very carefully – and ensure that the benefits outweigh the costs.

- you set clear objectives and design your roadshows around meeting these.

Depending on your roadshow – who it is aimed at, where it will go, how long it will last and what materials you already have – you may need to produce promotional literature and exhibition boards, as well as hiring a caravan.

TALKS AND SEMINARS

How better to promote your work than face-to-face? Talks and seminars offer you a perfect opportunity to reach out to an already interested audience, so take full advantage of them. Often organisations get asked to present a talk or workshop, and this provides you with a promotional platform. But don't just be reactive all the time. Try to get yourself invited to events to talk, and make this part of your promotional strategy. Also, organise your own events as part of your promotional work, where appropriate.

SPONSORSHIP

Most promotional work is not cheap; some is really expensive. Few charities have budgets large enough to do all the promotional work they would like, though many have been successful in attracting sponsorship to help stretch their budgets and allow them to take on projects that would otherwise be beyond their means.

Sponsorship is more important and more sophisticated now than ever before. Many television programmes now have sponsors, from Rumpole of the Bailey, which is sponsored by a port manufacturer, to Channel 4's Without Walls, which is supported by the organisation representing independent financial advisers. You can both sponsor (i.e. use it as your own promotional tool) and be sponsored as part of your marketing campaign.

> **TRUE STORY**
>
> *When Midland Bank reviewed its £1 million charitable budget, it realised that it was seeing very little return on its charitable giving. Businesses these days expect to see a return on their investment, even when it comes to charitable donations. Midland decided to make a bigger impact by supporting a smaller number of charities in key fields such as youth and disability. A shortlist of charities chosen by Midland was invited to tender. They were told what the Bank was looking for and had five weeks to come up with ideas for specific projects to meet Midland's requirements. They then had to pitch for the business. Shelter, noted for its professional marketing approach, learned in 1996 that it had been successful in pitching and was to receive £180,000 a year for three years as the Bank's main beneficiary. Shelter's marketing expertise paid off.*

Sponsoring Others

Sponsoring another body is a way of positioning your charity and promoting your name. You could perhaps sponsor a local football team if you needed to be seen as part of the community. Many voluntary organisations do this. Or you could consider sponsoring an important conference or research report. By being associated with something significant, high profile or prestigious, you can enjoy both reflected glory and positive media coverage.

Remember that if you plan to use sponsorship as part of your marketing strategy, you should ensure that your chosen project helps you meet your marketing aims. There's probably no point in sponsoring a children's painting competition at a village school if you are a large, national, London-based charity working with refugees. Why? Because however worthwhile the cause you are sponsoring, there needs to be something in it for you. You have to be clear from the outset about what you are getting out of it. Are you going to gain by association? Will it help you position your organisation? Find out before you commit yourself.

Seeking Sponsorship

Getting your organisation sponsored is obviously more difficult than offering sponsorship. Unless you already have both a high profile and a good reputation, it can be really difficult to find a sponsor for your organisation, though it is possible to attract project sponsorship. This is where a one-off campaign, publication or event is sponsored, as opposed to you being sponsored as an organisation. Some organisations have become so good at attracting sponsorship that they are in the enviable position of being able to ask companies to submit bids, with the highest bidder getting to associate themselves with the organisation. The public sector body Scottish Enterprise does this for its annual report, and has no difficulty in attracting a list of leading companies eager to pay for the privilege. In return they get a page of the report dedicated to them.

It is extremely unlikely that your charity will be so fortunate. Companies receive letters daily asking for money. Some receive thousands each year, with most only getting a standard "thanks but no thanks" reply. To increase your chances of successful sponsorship you need to take the following steps:

Ten Steps to Successful Sponsorship

1. Do your homework – find out who gives what to whom.

2. Approach only those organisations likely to consider supporting you – i.e. those with an established interest in the sort of work you do, those who have sponsored you (or a similar charity) in the past, or those with an obvious link (e.g. a car manufacturer and a road safety charity).

3. Phone up and get the name of the person to write to – letters to a named person are more likely to get to the right person (rather than getting lost in the bureaucracy of a large organisation) and they show that you have taken the care and trouble to find out.

4. Don't send the same letter to everyone – personalised letters stand a better chance of success.

TRUE STORY

Sponsors expect something in return for their sponsorship. RSPB have a corporate membership scheme which rewards supporters in various ways, such as by offering discounted advertising space in its Birds magazine. What can you offer that is tangible?

5. Keep your letter brief and persuasive.

6. Explain what's in it for the company – what they would get out of it and how it would enhance their image and help them with their business objectives.

7. Include any necessary background material, including your annual report.

8. If you can, time your approach for just before the sponsorship budget is allocated.

9. If you have missed this date, try again in the run-up to the year end, when many companies are distributing left-over money from their sponsorship budget.

10. If you are rejected, there is nothing to lose in politely contacting the company to find out why and to learn any lessons you can that will enable you to do better next time.

Setting up sponsorship deals is hard work and very time-consuming. You will get lots of rejections along the way, but don't lose heart or give up. Most good projects do, in the end, get support, but it does take stamina and a thick skin.

WHICH TOOL TO USE

In these last four chapters on promotional activity, we have looked at a wide range of promotional opportunities. Which should you opt for? There is no simple answer. It all depends on:

- what you are hoping to achieve.
- what your budget is.
- who you are trying to reach (your target audience).
- over what period of time you need to run a promotion.

It is likely that whatever you are doing, you will not rely on just one method. Let's say you are opening a hostel for homeless people. To promote it you might chose to:

- produce a leaflet on the service and leave copies at soup kitchens, in housing departments, at Citizens' Advice Bureaux (CABx) and other advice centres.
- write to professionals who work with homeless people, informing them of the service.
- have an opening event and seek editorial and broadcast coverage.

■ send a news release to the professional publications read by people in this field.

■ send a news release to the publications likely to be read by homeless people, such as the Big Issue, and/or advertise there.

■ produce a poster advertising the service and display it in places homeless people visit, such as DSS offices, housing association offices etc.

As you can see from the above example, the aim is to select methods that are cost effective and that will reach the target audience (in some cases, via an intermediary such as a homeless persons worker or a magazine advert).

TRUE STORY

The Health Education Authority needed an innovative way of publicising World Aids Day 1995 to one of its key target groups – young gay and heterosexual men. This group is a light user of the news media, so another way had to be found to reach it with the health promotion message. Given that two thirds of the two million people with access to the Internet are male, and two thirds are under the age of 34, this seemed the ideal vehicle. An attractive 'Web site' was established (containing Aids and HIV information), and a Red Ribbon screen save was produced for 'downloading' onto users' PCs – enabling the World Aids Day logo to have a presence on people's desks well after the event. Thanks to careful targeting and the right choice of promotional vehicle, the event was a great success for the HEA, with 200,000 people visiting the site.

DEVELOPING A MARKETING STRATEGY

What's in this chapter?

■ *how to develop your own marketing strategy.*
■ *setting objectives.*
■ *planning for the sort of organisation you would like to be.*
■ *doing a 'SWOT analysis'.*
■ *how to 'sell' the idea of marketing to sceptical colleagues.*
■ *evaluating marketing activity.*

By now you will be aware that marketing is multi-faceted. It is not simply about selling your services. To be effective at marketing you need to take a systematic and sustained approach. The marketing of your own organisation cannot be done in an ad hoc or casual way – a bit of marketing here, and a bit there. Marketing is an integrated approach, a way of working, and it must be planned and carried out in an organised way. You must also keep your marketing under review, and evaluate success (and failure) as part of that review. To work in this kind of planned way you need to have a clear strategy – a marketing strategy.

There is no simple way of developing a marketing strategy for your organisation, and there are no simple off-the-shelf answers or short-cuts. Marketing is time-consuming and requires long-term commitment. It is up to you to find an approach to developing a marketing strategy that suits your kind of organisation. You may like to take the approach set out below and to amend it to your own situation.

SHARED IDEAS

The best way of getting started with marketing is to involve others. Pull together a team comprising various 'stakeholders' in your organisation – committee members, staff, volunteers etc. This is your marketing team and they will be responsible for shaping your marketing strategy. Each will have a different viewpoint, which is part of the strength of the group. Its many perspectives will ensure that your ideas are questioned and challenged.

It is important that your team understands its role – and understands exactly what marketing is about. You will probably need to hold an information and discussion seminar to make sure that you are all starting from the same knowledge base, with a clear understanding of marketing and its use for your organisation.

HOW TO GET STARTED

You need to set objectives for your marketing activity, so that you have a clear idea of what you are trying to achieve, and so you can monitor and evaluate progress. However, before you can set objectives, you need to carry out a review of where you are and what the current position is. To do this, get your marketing group to start by examining where your charity is now. This involves looking critically and objectively at how you operate, why you take the decisions you do, what influences your work. You need to look at your market, your products, your customers, and your promotional work. In short you are aiming for an understanding of how you currently work and the factors in your operating environment that affect that work.

Only after you have done all this can you focus on where you want to go and on what sort of an organisation you would like to be in, say, five years' time. This is where your objectives come in. The way you get there is your strategy.

YOUR MARKET

You operate within a market, and you need to understand that market if you are to be successful in it. In looking at your market you need to consider:

a. the external variables over which you have no control (which political party is in power, locally or nationally, for example).

b. the internal variables over which you have complete control (the set up/structure of your organisation, for example).

This will enable you to have a clear picture of the factors you can influence, and those which will inevitably limit you. Refer back to Chapter Four for more information on the factors you need to consider.

It is useful at this stage to carry out a 'SWOT analysis'. SWOT is an acronym which stands for:

Strengths – What are you good at as an organisation? What do you do better than others?

Weaknesses – What are you poor at? Where is there room for improvement?

Opportunities – What opportunities are there for you externally, either now or in the future?

Threats – What threats exist externally, now or in the future? Who are your competitors and what threats do they pose?

As part of your strategy you will need to make assumptions about the future market, including the actions of your competitors. You will need to be aware that you must build upon your strengths, strengthen your weak areas, take action to minimise threats and ensure that you grasp opportunities.

YOUR CUSTOMERS

In considering your customers start by listing who they are. Next examine what they want from you. Finally, take a realistic look at what you can offer. Remember that meeting customer needs may involve changing your organisation so it is better suited to meeting those needs (i.e. altering internal variables) as well as recognising the constraints imposed by external variables over which you have no control, and working to provide the best that you can given these factors.

Looking in turn at each customer type, what are their three main needs? Here's an example: the main needs of the social work department may be to find an organisation that can provide:

1. a professional and high quality community care service.

2. one that is also cost-effective, but does not compromise on quality.

3. a service that is accountable, open and involves residents and relatives.

Another example. The main needs of shoppers in a charity shop may be:

1. to shop in a bright and cheerful place – they do not want dank and smelly shops they are embarrassed to be seen in.

2. to find a good choice of clean, fashionable clothes.

3. to be able to afford the prices.

You can only begin to meet needs once you understand what those needs are. You will probably find in going back to basics – looking at what your customers actually need, as opposed to what you give them – that research may be required. You may want to ask your customers what they would like from you, what their needs and priorities are. Chapter Six will help guide you through the research maze.

You must understand what is really important to your customers when they buy. For example, is there a rule which says that the council will only buy care services from organisations where staff have a social work qualification? If so, there is no point in developing such services unless you can fulfil this need from your main customer. If your customers buy from your mail order catalogue because doing so fulfils an emotional need, you need to recognise this and reflect this need in the copy and design of your future catalogues.

WHAT NEXT?

Getting started is always the hardest bit. Once you have reviewed where you are now, and worked out where you would like to be, draw up some short-term (perhaps covering the following 12 months) and some long-term (up to five years ahead) objectives. Your objectives should state very clearly what you hope to achieve. Having done all this, you are ready to work on your strategy – in other words, on the details of how you will achieve your objectives. Draw on the ideas presented in the previous chapters to help you meet your objectives. Look at your marketing mix. See how much time and effort need to be put into modifying your products. How much money can you afford to promote them? Who are you promoting them to and how? Don't forget 'place' and 'price'. Consider all the elements of marketing and see how each one may have a role in helping you do what you do better.

> **TRUE STORY**
>
> *All organisations need a clear strategy that is well thought-out and thoroughly researched. In the Christmas period before the launch of Great Ormond Street's 'Wishing Well' Appeal, the charity was offered a £1 million fundraising campaign by a major newspaper. Many charities would jump at such an offer, but the Wishing Well Appeal had a clear marketing and fundraising strategy into which the offer simply did not fit. The organisers were concerned that if they accepted, the public would say: "Oh, we gave to that last year." Eventually the Appeal raised £54m -£24m more than the target.*

EVALUATION

You need to evaluate your work, and your marketing strategy should explain how this will be done. Traditional measures in business/commerce have included measurables such as increased sales, profits, reduced costs, advertising effectiveness etc. Some of these are very useful to voluntary organisations, such as advertising effectiveness (it would be wrong of a charity to waste donors' money on ineffective advertising). Some are not. For voluntary organisations there is a whole set of other measures that are often a great deal more important than profit: for example, the social benefits of a service, the social need, the cost to society of not running the service etc.

Social Need: It might be very expensive to run a free condom service for prostitutes, and a commercial organisation interested only in profit would be unable to operate it if their bottom line is the balance sheet. However, the price of not running such a service might prove too costly in social terms, leading to the spread of HIV/AIDS among adults, the birth of HIV positive babies, and the transmission of a variety of sexual diseases.

Social benefits: The operation of a service to rehabilitate joy riders and to encourage them not to reoffend could be cost effective not in financial terms, but in terms of social benefit.

Developing a marketing strategy is only half of your task. The other half involves 'selling' the concept of marketing to others within your organisation. If you do not do this, all your hard work on the strategy may be wasted. For marketing to work, you need a marketing organisation, and that involves bringing everyone on board. But how?

'SELLING' MARKETING TO YOUR COLLEAGUES

Many people are very sceptical when it comes to marketing. There are probably people in your organisation who do not understand properly what it is, and may believe that your charity is wrong to invest in something that may appear an expensive luxury. If you are to be a successful marketing-led charity, it is important that others in the organisation understand what marketing is and why it is so important to you. They need to take it seriously, contribute to the marketing debate, and support marketing initiatives. To bring about an attitude like this in your organisation, you will have to work hard and steadily. You cannot expect others to jump up and down with excitement, you must foster that enthusiasm. In short you must 'sell' the idea of marketing within your charity.

How you set about this will depend on:

- the size of your organisation.
- the age of your organisation.
- the sorts of people involved in your organisation.
- the amount of marketing-type activity you have undertaken in the past.

Clearly it is an easier task 'selling' marketing to a small, young organisation with go-ahead people than to a large, traditional, paternalistic and bureaucratic dinosaur of a charity! Whatever your organisation, you need to:

- explain to everyone what marketing is and why it is important.
- involve a representative group (of staff, volunteers, committee members etc.) in developing the marketing strategy.
- ensure that the main points of the strategy are communicated to others within the organisation.

When it comes to explaining what marketing is, employ the marketing techniques in this book to get the message across. This might include an article in the staff newsletter, a talk at a staff meeting, a roadshow (in larger, more spread out organisations), or simply a memo to all staff. The same methods can be used to communicate the final strategy, and you may also wish to produce a short leaflet outlining the key points and indicating what everyone's role is in being a marketing-led organisation.

Be careful not to get technical when talking about marketing; it is a sure-fire way of switching people off. If you want to sell the notion of marketing, use plain language and arguments that people can relate to and understand. The key points you need to get across will be:

■ marketing is not selling.

■ marketing involves being needs-led, not resource driven. In other words, a marketing approach is entirely in harmony with what most charities exist for: meeting need.

■ marketing is about listening to users and taking action on their views, providing the services that are required.

When put across like this, it will be hard for staff not to see marketing's relevance. You can explain to doubters that marketing is needed because:

■ your service-users are generally not in the privileged position of being able to shop around for the service that suits. It is therefore all the more important that you take the time to find out exactly what your users require. Marketing techniques can help you find out what users want.

■ you probably have far more 'customers' than you can cope with. In a situation where demand outstrips supply (e.g. for affordable housing, cheap nursery provision, Third World aid etc.) it is easier for voluntary organisations to deliver a second rate service. A marketing-led approach will ensure that you avoid this and strive for excellence.

■ limited resources and tight budgets are common in voluntary organisations, and this can lead to charities developing services and products that meet the budget rather than satisfy the need. Marketing-led organisations do not fall into the trap of being resource-driven (though naturally they have to work within their budgets).

KEEP WORKING AT IT

'Selling' marketing is not a one-off activity; you need to keep marketing awareness alive in your organisation. So having initially persuaded everyone that marketing is a good and necessary activity, you need to feed their interest. Share marketing successes with staff, get them to contribute ideas and feedback, and encourage people to think marketing at every turn. Do all this and you will have a truly marketing-led organisation that attracts the necessary funding to deliver the quality services that your users need and want. And that is, after all, what you were set up to do!

CHAPTER THIRTEEN

A PLAIN ENGLISH GUIDE TO MARKETING JARGON

Marketing jargon can be impenetrable to the outsider. The aim of this glossary is to give you a reference point. If you are reading other marketing books (see appendix for reading list), you can refer to this user-friendly definition of terms to help you. Many of the terms and concepts outlined below are dealt with in more detail in the relevant chapters of this book. Note that terms are not listed alphabetically; they are grouped together with related terms. See the index for an alphabetical list.

GENERAL MARKETING JARGON

Cause-related Marketing

A company with an image, product or service to sell builds a relationship or partnership with a 'cause' or a number of 'causes' for mutual benefit. Cadbury's 'Strollerthon' – an annual sponsored mass-participation walk through London – is an example of this. Save the Children benefits from the cash raised from the event, while Cadbury's gets publicity, goodwill, a database of participants and a chance to give out product samples at the event. In 1994, for example, Save the Children got £250,000 from the Strollerthon, and subsequent research revealed that 52% of walkers perceived Cadbury's as a caring company.

Marketing Mix

The term 'marketing mix' refers to the four Ps – **product**, **price**, **place** and **promotion** – and it is important to know which of the Ps are the key influencing factors for your market.

Product

We tend to think of products as things – such as a tin of baked beans or a packet of washing powder. "Product" here refers to your product or service. It might be a product proper, such as second hand clothing, if you run a charity shop, or a publication or handbook if you run a support service for voluntary organisations. Selling the product may involve an exchange of money. Or it could be that your 'product' is a free service, such as counselling, a drop-in centre, a welfare rights clinic – or one of a host of other services run by charities and voluntary organisations in Britain.

Price

If you are selling products, such as third world crafts, Nicaraguan coffee or second hand clothes, your products will have a price tag on them. It is not so straightforward with services. Take a youth cafe, for example. What's the price of a cup of coffee? Is it the 10p you charge, or the 30p it costs you to make it, when you take into account rent, rates, staff costs etc.? Is the cost the £40,000 you get each year from the council to run the cafe, or the 15p you charge for a cheese roll? It is both of these things. Part of your operation is selling food and drinks to young people, and it is important that you get the price right. Another part of your operation is providing a drop-in service to local young people, which is paid for by the council; you need to price this service right, too, otherwise the council may feel that they are not getting good value for money.

Place

Place is the bridge that connects buyers and sellers. It ensures that the product and customer are brought together, thus creating an opportunity for the customer to buy. In conventional marketing 'place' refers to distribution – getting the products to the places where they can be available to consumers. If you make baked beans, you need a distribution system that enables you to get your tins out of the factory and into the shops where they will be sold. Clearly in manufacturing the 'place' P is a really important one; tins of baked beans stacked in a factory are of no use to anyone – they need to be placed where they can be bought. 'Place' when used to describe distribution is of use to some charities, for example those which make a product. But it also has a use, as a concept, to service-providers. Just as those making a product need to know how to get it to the customer, you too need to consider how to get the consumer to your service. Is your drop-in centre on a bus route, for example? For fundraisers, too, place is an issue, for they need to ensure that collecting tins are in the right places and that the distribution system operates to collect them up again. Fundraising envelopes and leaflets need to get through the right doors. So even here, 'place' has its role in the marketing mix.

Promotion

This is the aspect of marketing that we most readily associate the word with. Indeed, this is often what we mean when we talk about marketing. Promotion involves promoting your service or product, but the question is, "Promote it to whom?" Are you promoting it to the people who use it or those who pay for it? Those who use are not always those who pay, even in the commercial sector. Children's pasta products, for example, are paid for by adults, but advertising for Postman Pat spaghetti is not aimed at them; it is targeted at children, as they are the major influencing factor on how and what food is bought in a household. Supermarket chain Asda did some research into consumer buying habits and discovered that children exert a strong influence over what their parents buy in supermarkets, to the tune of almost £2 billion a year. But back to the voluntary sector; promotion involves promoting to the user of your service – teenagers, for example, in the case of the youth club – as well as funders. The council who pay for the youth club need to be as convinced about its use to the town's youth as young people need to be persuaded that it is a place worth going to. The promotional tools used and the messages promoted will differ, but the need for promotion to both audiences remains. Promotion involves advertising, leaflets, posters and other methods to reach target audiences.

Five New Ps

In 1981 a further three Ps were suggested for service industries: **People** (the attitude of staff, behaviour, training, commitment etc.); **Physical Evidence** (the surroundings in which a service takes place, its furnishings and decor, noise levels, layout etc.); and **Process** (policies, procedures etc.). In 1994 a further P was suggested by charity marketing expert Ian Bruce: **Philosophy**. This refers to a charity's way of doing things, its beliefs and guiding principles. Norman Hart, Britain's first professor of PR, suggests that P for '**Perception**' should be added to the classic four Ps.

Market Segmentation

To be effective you need to 'know your market.' That makes it sound as if you have just one market, made up of one type of person. It is important to recognise that not all markets are uniform. Most are made up of sub-groups or segments. You need to spot the segments in your market and identify what makes one different and distinct from another, and to tailor your approach for these distinct markets. For example, an examination of your donor base might reveal that it is elderly people who leave legacies to your charity, so the style of copy and design for your legacy pack might be different from that for your payroll giving leaflet, which research tells you is most popular with younger people. Spotting the sub-groups in your market is called market segmentation. Your market might be segmented **geographically** (if you have clear regional differences, for example); **demographically** (sex, age, lifecycle or family size); **socio-economically** (income, occupation, social class etc.); **psychographically** (in other words, according to the type of person who gives, their personality or lifestyle, for example); and/or **behaviouristically** (how often they give/buy from you, what they look for from you etc.).

Market Penetration

This is where you take your existing products to your existing markets. Your aim is to capture a bigger share of this market, or to reach previously unreached potential customers.

Market Development

Here you take your existing products, but you promote them to new target markets.

Product Development

This is where you develop brand new products, but offer them to your existing target markets.

Diversification

This involves complete change. You are developing new products and offering them to new markets, a risky strategy for charities and businesses alike.

Niche Markets

A niche market is one that is small and specialist, for example skate-boarding computer whizzkids. In business it can be very profitable to cater for niche markets, as they are generally not targeted by anyone else and therefore are crying out for products or services to meet their needs. Often they are prepared to pay handsomely, and with no competition the way is open for companies to make good profits. Many charities cater for niche markets. A charity providing a specialist service for fathers who have lost a child could be said to be catering for a niche. By dealing with something that does not affect a great many people, and by offering a service where currently there may be a gap, a case could be made to funders that you are meeting a very specialist need. If no one else is doing anything quite like you, you could stand a good chance of getting funds. On the other hand, pioneers often find it difficult to attract funding, and projects for minority groups can find it more difficult than those catering for a mass market. Equally, you are more vulnerable, as are businesses catering for niches. If something happens to your niche, or another player (competitor) appears, you could find that you have no other market to provide services to, or that your skills are so specialised that you cannot diversify.

Niche Products

A niche product is simply a product or service developed to meet the needs of a particular niche market (see above).

SWOT Analysis

SWOT is an acronym. It stands for:
Strengths: what you are good at, what you do well, what factors are in your favour

Weaknesses: what you are poor at, what factors are against you

Opportunities: what external opportunities there are for you to develop new services or to attract new funding etc.

Threats: what external threats could affect you – new legislation or competition, or a change in government, for example

A SWOT analysis is simply an examination of your organisation's strengths and weaknesses, and the opportunities and threats which it faces. Once you have carried out a SWOT analysis, you can start to build on your strengths and, where appropriate, do something to address your weaknesses. Remember that a threat to one organisation can be an opportunity to another. The National Lottery has been seen as a threat to some of the big charities, whose donations have dropped since its launch. Conversely the Lottery has opened up a new source of funding which many smaller charities are benefiting from.

USP

This is an acronym for **Unique Selling Point** (sometimes also called 'unique selling proposition') – it is the thing that differentiates you from all the others. For example, there might be scores of children's charities, but your USP is that you are the only one set up exclusively to care for dying children in Sutcliffeville. No one else is offering that service. It is what makes you stand apart from the rest.

MARKETING RESEARCH JARGON

Demographics

This relates to population characteristics such as age, sex and family size.

Donor Profile

A donor profile paints a picture of the sort of person who supports your organisation – for example, middle-aged Christian Guardian readers with two incomes, grown-up children, living in the south of England and interested in the Arts.

Methodology

This is jargon for how you intend to get the information you need. For example, you may decide to use a postal questionnaire plus depth interviews with a sample of donors.

Primary Data

Primary data is not ready-made. You have to gather it yourself, or commission someone else to do it for you. It is thus more expensive and potentially much more time-consuming than secondary data (see below).

Secondary Data

Secondary data is material that already exists (as opposed to primary data, which you gather yourself). It includes, for example, government publications and statistics (e.g. the Census of Population, the Family Expenditure Survey, reports from the Registrar General, Monthly Digest of Statistics and Social Trends). Large reference libraries are an obvious starting point when tracking down secondary data.

Samples

With the exception of the government's ten-yearly census, no survey can cover the whole of the population. Researchers use instead a 'sample', which is a smaller group that is representative of the 'population' they wish to survey. By surveying a representative sample, rather than the entire relevant population, your survey is made more manageable and affordable.

ADVERTISING JARGON

Above the Line

This is an advertising term which refers to paid-for advertising using press, radio, TV, cinema and billboards.

Below the Line

This refers to advertising and promotion via media other than 'above the line' media – such as direct mail, exhibitions, promotional brochures and give-aways (such as promotional pens, balloons and key rings).

Advertising Rate Card

Newspaper and magazine advertising departments produce a rate card which sets out what an advertisement costs according to where it is in the publication, its size, whether it is colour or black and white, etc. It also contains production information such as deadlines and the form in which you need to submit your advert.

BRAD (British Rate And Data)

This monthly publication (which can be consulted at large reference libraries) sets out the advertising rates of a wide range of publications, from daily newspapers to women's and special interest magazines. It also contains circulation information (see below).

Circulation

Circulation figures tell you how many people buy a particular publication. 'Readership' figures tell you how many people read a publication. Usually readership figures are higher than circulation ones; a newspaper or magazine will frequently be read by more than just the person who bought it.

Classified Adverts or 'Smalls'

These are small adverts which comprise lines of text. There is no design element. They are usually charged by the line, so advertisers abbreviate their copy to fit as many words in per line.

Display Adverts

These are creative adverts which have been professionally designed.

Facing Matter

This is when your advert is placed alongside editorial, rather than being buried in an advertising section surrounded by other adverts.

Recall Tests

Recall tests are used in advertising research to see how many of a sample of respondents remember having seen an advert.

Run-of-Paper

You do not get to choose where in the publication your advert appears; it is placed at the publisher's discretion.

Special Position Adverts

You can specify if you want your advert to appear in a special position, such as the front page or near the leader column. If you are running a charity to build schools in the third world, you may opt for your advert to be placed on the education page. The price of your advert will depend on where in the paper it is placed. There can be a waiting list for the best positions, as these are often booked up in advance.

Solus Position

There will be no other advertisements adjacent to your own. This means it will not have to compete for attention with other adverts.

Single Column Centimetre (scc)

This is the unit of vertical measurement that is used to measure the size of an advert and therefore its cost.

DIRECT MAIL JARGON

ACORN

This acronym stands for **A Classification Of Residential Neighbourhoods**. It classifies people and households according the type of neighbourhood they live in. People in a particular neighbourhood will probably share similar lifestyles, social characteristics and behaviour. There are 38 different neighbourhood types and 11 different 'family group classifications.' Using the information it is possible to produce mailing lists that will enable you to target very precisely so that you can reach only 'high-status, non-family' areas, or 'unmodernised terraced houses with old people.' There is a similar system called MOSAIC.

Active Customer/Member/Subscriber

Generally an active customer is one who has purchased from you, joined your organisation or sent for information from you within the last 12 months. Many charities keep lists of active customers so that they can mail them during fundraising appeals.

Co-op Mailings

This is when two or more non-competitive organisations come together and have their information or promotional material inserted into the one mailing. By sharing the costs it is a cost-effective exercise.

Cost Per Conversion

You add together all the costs of a direct mail campaign and divide by the number of orders received/donations made/subscriptions taken out. This gives you your cost per conversion and it is a good way of working out whether your campaign has been a success in terms of the response it generated.

Door Drops

These are unaddressed mail packs or leaflets delivered to households by hand, not in the mail. Strictly speaking this is not direct mail, it is direct advertising.

Friend of a Friend

This is when an existing supporter/donor/member sends in the name of a friend or relative who may be interested in receiving information from you. This technique is used a lot by commercial organisations, who offer incentives to people to get them to send in details of friends. It can sometimes be an effective way of building up a mailing list of interested people.

List Cleaning

Mailing lists need to be kept up to date if they are to be of any use. List cleaning involves correcting names and addresses, removing those who have moved away or those who have not responded to your mail within a designated period (e.g. after four mailings or within one month).

Mailing House

You can arrange to have your direct mail addressed, collated and despatched by a mailing house.

MOSAIC

See ACORN above.

Gone-Aways

This is a term used to refer to mail returned by the Royal Mail to the sender because the intended recipient has gone away or the address is wrong or non-existent. Such mail is also known as 'returns'. Gone-aways are a waste of money: when you get one you must update/amend your mailing list accordingly.

Piggy Backs

A piggy back is when you enclose your literature in another organisation's existing mailing, for example by inserting a flier into another charity's newsletter. This is a cheaper way of doing a mailing. Charities can make money this way too, by offering a piggy back service in their own mailings.

MEDIA RELATIONS JARGON

News Releases

Sometimes referred to as 'press releases', they are stories written in newspaper style by PR people. Releases are issued by companies and organisations to the media in the hope of securing press or broadcast coverage for a story.

Press or News Conferences

This is an event held specially for the media to brief them on an important issue, a new product or service, or something that is generally very newsworthy. If you can achieve the same effect simply by issuing a news release, do not go to the trouble of holding a news conference.

Press Officers

Press officers are in-house specialists who deal with media relations and are a contact point for journalists seeking information. Many charities employ a press officer.

Media Invitations

If you want to let the media know about an event, news conference or photocall, issue them with a media invitation setting out briefly what is happening, where, when and why.

Photocalls

If you are organising an event and are seeking publicity for it, consider whether it has 'photo opportunity' potential. If so, set up a photocall, where you invite newspaper photographers (and possibly television, too) to attend at a certain time to take pictures. Invite them by issuing a media invitation (see above) – sometimes also known as a photocall notice.

Press or Media Statement

If you are asked by the media to comment on something, or to answer questions on a particular issue, you might find that you are unable or unwilling to do an interview. By issuing a press statement – a written response – you can avoid an interview while at the same time getting your point across.

Press Cuttings Bureaux

These companies will send you cuttings on your charity from a massive range of publications. They are expensive, as they charge a reading fee and an amount per cutting, so are suitable only for very large charities doing a lot of media work, or for one-off, high profile campaigns.

Broadcast Monitoring Companies

A number of companies specialise in monitoring radio and television output, and can ring you up to alert you that you have had a mention. They can also provide transcripts of programmes and video and audio tapes. Again they are expensive, but can be useful for the bigger charities.

Journalist/Reporter

There are specialist reporters or correspondents (such as housing, health and local government correspondents) and general reporters who have to write about a very wide range of issues but who may specialise in none.

Chief Reporter

As the name suggests, the chief reporter is more senior than other reporters and generally gets the best and most interesting assignments. They are usually more experienced than other reporters on the paper.

News Editor

The news editor selects the news, decides where in the paper it will appear, and assigns reporters to follow up particular stories.

Sub Editor

Cutting stories to fit the space and headline-writing are two of the main responsibilities of the sub.

Editor

This is the top job on a newspaper. On larger papers it is generally a management job rather than a hands-on writing position, although the editor often writes a leader or comment column. On small papers and free papers, the editor can also be a reporter of sorts. The editor is responsible for the content, tone and style of a newspaper.

CHAPTER FOURTEEN

USEFUL ADDRESSES

This is far from a comprehensive list, though it covers the main companies and organisations you may need to contact, as well as the key marketing magazines and handbooks. (Further reading can be found in the appendix which follows this chapter.)

MARKETING

The Chartered Institute of Marketing

Moor Hall
Cookham
Maidenhead
Berks SL6 9QH
Tel. 01628–852310

The CIM was established in 1911 and has over 50,000 members. It is a membership organisation offering a range of services including training, professional qualifications, a library and information service, and consultancy. It produces various publications, including a journal, newsletters and marketing reports. The CIM has regional offices at:

29 St Vincent Place
Glasgow G1 2DT

Tel. 0141–221 7700

Chamber of Commerce House
22 Great Victoria Street
Belfast BT2 7BJ

Tel. 01232–244113

Eaton Place Business Centre
114 Washway Road
Sale
Cheshire M33 7RF

Tel. 0161–905 1458

Marketing

Haymarket Publications
PO Box 219
Woking
Surrey GU21 1LZ

Tel. 01483 776345

A weekly marketing newspaper.

Marketing Week

Centaur Communications
St Giles House
50 Poland Street
London W1V 4AX

Tel. 0171–439 4222

A weekly marketing magazine.

Marketing Pocket Book

NTC Publications
Farm Road
Henley-on-Thames
Oxfordshire RG9 1EJ

Tel. 01491–411000

This pocket book is published annually for the Advertising Association by NTC Publications and costs £16.95. It contains a vast array of marketing information covering a wide range of subjects.

ADVERTISING

The Advertising Standards Authority

2 Torrington Place
London WC1E 7HW

Tel. 0171–580 5555

Established in 1962, the ASA provides independent scrutiny of the advertising industry. It investigates complaints and ensures that the system operates in the public interest. It is independent both of government and the advertising industry.

The Committee of Advertising Practice

2 Torrington Place
London WC1E 7HW

Tel. 0171--580 5555

The CAP is the self regulatory body that devises and enforces the British Codes of Advertising and Sales Promotion. These are reproduced in a free guide, available from the above address. CAP also offers free copy advice on your advertising and promotions, to help you ensure it meets the codes. Ring 0171-580 4100.

The Incorporated Society of British Advertisers Limited

44 Hertford Street
London W1Y 8AE

Tel. 0171–499 7502

ISBA represents the interests of the majority of British advertisers. It can offer organisations help with selecting advertising, promotional and direct marketing agencies, and offers training and a range of useful publications and briefing papers.

Advertising Agency Register

26 Market Place
London W1

Tel. 0171–437 3357

This independent organisation will give you the names of advertising agencies suitable for your brief.

Campaign Magazine

Haymarket Publications
PO Box 219
Woking
Surrey GU21 1LZ

Tel. 01483–776345

A weekly publication focusing on the advertising industry.

BUS ADVERTISING

Buspak (UK) Limited

11 Empress Business Centre
Chester Road
Old Trafford
Manchester M16 9EB

Tel. 0161–877 7414

To make contact by telephone call the operator on 100 and ask for Freephone Buspak. This is one of the largest bus advertising companies in the country. It can arrange for you to advertise on buses in your area or nationally.

BUS TICKET ADVERTISING

Image Promotions

Units 2&3 Maple Works
Old Shoreham Road
Hove
East Sussex BN3 7ED

Tel. 01273–726325

Image Promotions has organised over 95% of all bus ticket promotions in the UK, though as yet has not done one for a charity. It has links with over 100 bus companies in all major towns and cities. The company can help you with planning and advice, bus company bookings and liaison, artwork and design, printing, delivery and campaign monitoring.

MARKET RESEARCH

The Market Research Society

15 Northburgh Street
London EC1V 0AH

Tel. 0171–490 4911

Founded in 1946, the Market Research Society is the professional association for those involved in compiling or using research. It has around 7,500 members and offers them a monthly magazine and quarterly journal. The Society produces an annual training programme which includes such courses as Questionnaire Design, Marketing Skills, and Training the Interviewer Trainer. Courses are open to non-members, though a higher fee is charged. They also produce a free directory of organisations providing market research services.

Raymead

13 College Park
Eastfield Road
Peterborough PE1 4AW

Tel. 01733–61799

Raymead sell software to help you set up databases that will enable you to have a clearer picture of your customers.

Crossbow Research

Aviary Court
138 Miles Road
Epsom KT19 9AB

Tel. 01372–725400

This company specialises in market research for voluntary organisations and comes highly recommended by a number of charities.

GENERAL RESEARCH

Press Association Library

85 Fleet Street
London EC4P 4BE

Tel. 0171–353 7440

This library holds over 14 million news cuttings on every subject from 1926 onwards.

British Library Newspaper Library

Colindale Avenue
London NW9 5HE

Tel. 0171–323 7535

English, Scottish, Welsh and Irish newspapers from 1700 are housed here.

Equal Opportunities Commission Library

Overseas House
Quay Street
Manchester M3 3HN

Tel. 0161–833 9244

Books, pamphlets and press cuttings on equal opportunities.

Health Information Library

Marylebone Library
Marylebone Road
London NW1 5PS

Tel. 0171–798 1039

Books, pamphlets and periodicals on all aspects of health services and medicine.

Office of Population Censuses and Surveys Library

St Catherine's House
10 Kingsway
London WC2B 6JP

Tel. 0171–396 2238

DIRECT MAIL

The Direct Marketing Association

Haymarket House
1 Oxendon Street
London SW1Y 4EE

Tel. 0171–321 2525

This body represents the direct marketing industry. It produces a code of practice and a list of accredited list brokers.

The Institute of Direct Marketing

1 Park Road
Teddington Middlesex TW11 0AR

Tel. 0181–977 5705

The IDM organises educational initiatives, including the Direct Marketing Diploma, to improve the knowledge of direct marketing.

The Direct Mail Services Standards Board

26 Eccleston Street
London SW1W 9PY

Tel. 0171–824 8651

The DMSSB provides a list of approved suppliers and confers recognised status on suppliers who meet the highest ethical and professional standards.

Direct Mail Accreditation and Recognition Centre

4th Floor
248 Tottenham Court Road
London W1P 9AD

Tel. 0171–631 0904

Established in 1995, DMARC is an accreditation scheme to ensure direct mail suppliers adhere to the best practices and self-regulatory guidelines of the industry.

On-line Professional Resources Direct Marketing Selector

http://www.demon.co.uk/onpro

This is an electronic directory for people involved in direct marketing. It lists, for example, mailing list owners and mailing houses, as well as other relevant services. It can be accessed freely by anyone on the Internet.

AM&M Direct

Studio 3/3
Chelsea Harbour Yard
London SW10 0XD

Tel. 0171–376 5727

This company specialises in charity direct mail, especially fundraising mailings.

Royal Mail Mailsort

This is a Royal Mail service which offers discounts (ranging from 13% to 32%) for large mailings sorted by you. If you are sending at least 4,000 letters in one go, and you can sort them geographically, you could get a good discount. Talk to your local Sales Centre on 0345-950 950 for details. Royal Mail offer a range of services to support direct mail campaigns, including Freepost, Business Reply and Door to Door. Ask them for details. They also produce a useful Direct Mail Guide.

Precision Marketing

Centaur Communications
St Giles House
50 Poland Street
London W1V 4AX

Tel. 0171–439 4222

A weekly direct marketing magazine.

Marketing Direct

Haymarket Business Publications
30 Lancaster Gate
London W2 3LP

Tel. 0181–845 7149

A monthly magazine on direct marketing.

MAILING LISTS

There are many different mailing list companies, and this is by no means comprehensive.

AM&M Direct

Studio 3/3
Chelsea Harbour Yard
London SW10 0XD

Tel. 0171–376 5727

AM&M Direct offer a range of services to charities, including their Charity Donor Prospects List, which lists over 300,000 people suitable for charity mailings. They say theirs is the best performing list in the country for charity donor acquisition mailings.

MarketScan

8 Duke's Court
Chichester
West Sussex PO19 2FX

Tel. 01243–786711

MarketScan will also assemble and post mailings for you. And they can arrange 'shared' mailings, where you share your mailing with one or more non-competing organisations. This can more than halve your costs.

Financial Times Business Lists

5th Floor
Number One Southwark Bridge
London SE1 9HL

Tel. 0171–873 3000

Royal Mail Address Management Centre

4 St George's Business Centre
St George's Square
Portsmouth PO1 3AX

Tel. 01705–838515

Royal Mail have an address management database on CD ROM called PAF, the Postcode Address File. It contains 25 million addresses and allows you to cross reference with census information, local authority ward codes etc. or to check addresses are correct before adding them to mailing lists.

The Direct Mail Information Service

5 Carlisle Street
London W1V 5RG

Tel. 0171–494 0483

For industry statistics, research and general information on direct mail, contact the DMIS.

DMA Directory of List Owners, Brokers, Managers and Builders

The Direct Marketing Association
Haymarket House
1 Oxendon Street
London SW1Y 4EE

Tel. 0171–321 2525

This body represents the direct marketing industry. It offers a list brokering advisory service.

BRAD Direct Marketing Lists, Rates and Data

Maclean Hunter House
Chalk Lane
Cockfosters Road
Barnet
Hertfordshire EN4 0BU

Tel. 0181–242 3132

This is a guide to lists and direct mail services. It costs around £200 annually.

Mailing Preference Service

Freepost 22
London W1E 7EZ

Tel. 0171–738 1625

Members of the public can register their details with the MPS to help cut down on the amount of 'junk mail' they receive. The MPS produces a list of everyone who has contacted them to say that they do not want to receive unsolicited mail, and this list is made available to list owners, who then remove these people from their lists. Hopefully this makes everyone happy: consumers do not get unwanted mail and companies do not waste money writing to people who have no interest. You can buy a copy of this list for £100 plus VAT.

Telephone Preference Service

This is a similar service to the one outlined above, only it covers direct marketing via the telephone. It is supported by, among others, the Institute of Charity Fundraising Managers and the Direct Marketing Association. Ring British Telecom for details.

The Office of the Data Protection Registrar

Wycliffe House
Water Lane
Wilmslow
SK9 5AX

Tel. 01625–535777

PROMOTIONAL MERCHANDISE

The British Promotional Merchandise Association

Suite 12
4th Floor
Parkway House
Sheen Lane
London SW14 8LS

Tel. 0181–878 0825

Promotions News

Published six times a year, this is the newspaper of the BPMA (see above). It is full of adverts from companies publicising the promotional items they produce. These range from cheap biros, balloons and carrier bags right through to tasteful branded gifts and fundraising items.

Rocket Badge Company

Byron Mews
114 Shirland Road
London W9 2BT

Tel. 0171–289 3262

Producing a wide range of badges, this company works for a number of charities and offers registered charities a discount.

Mainline Promotions

Collins Court
High Street
Cranleigh
Surrey GU6 8AS

Tel. 01483–271171

This company produces promotional textiles, clothing and bags and has worked for a number of charities.

Craft Emblems

Aspen House
14 Station Road
Kettering
Northants NN15 7HE

Tel. 01536–513501

Craft Emblems will source a variety of promotional items and specialise in charity work.

London Cardguide Limited

68 Brewer Street
London W1R 3PJ

Tel. 0171–494 2229

This company pioneered the idea of promotional postcards. They will produce postcards and distribute them to selected cafés and restaurants across Britain.

PUBLIC RELATIONS

The Institute of Public Relations

The Old Trading House
15 Northburgh Street
London EC1V 0PR

Tel. 0171–235 5151

This is the professional body which represents around 5,000 PR professionals.

The Public Relations Consultants Association

Willow House
Willow Place
Victoria
London SW1P 1JH

Tel. 0171–233 6026

The PRCA can help you find a PR consultancy, for they run a free referral service, though they will only recommend their members, who tend to be the more expensive consultancies.

IPR Journal

This monthly publication is published by the IPR.

PR Week

174 Hammersmith Road
London W6 7JP
Tel. 0171–413 4520

The weekly magazine for people working in PR. Covers charity and public sector as well as business PR issues.

PRESS CUTTINGS BUREAUX

Romeike and Curtice

Hale House
290-296 Green Lanes
London N13 5TP

Tel. 0181–882 0155

Durrant's Press Cuttings

103 Whitecross Street
London EC1Y 8QT

Tel. 0171–588 3671

The Broadcast Monitoring Company

891/2 Worship Street
London EC2A 2BE

Tel. 0171–247 1166

EDS Presscuttings

25-27 Easton Street
London WC1X 0DS

Tel. 0171–278 8441

McCallum Media Monitor

65 St. Vincent Crescent
Glasgow G3 8FQ

Tel. 0141–221 1795

Paperclip Partnership

Unit 9
The Ashway Centre
Elm Crescent
Kingston-upon-Thames
Surrey KT2 6HH

Tel. 0181–549 4857

All of the above offer a national service and some have local offices.

We Find It (Press Clippings)

103 South Parade
Belfast BT7 2GN

Tel. 01232–646008

Specialises in Northern Ireland newspapers and magazines.

BROADCAST MONITORING

The Broadcast Monitoring Company

89 plus a half Worship Street
London EC2A 2BE

Tel. 0171–247 1166

Tellex Monitors

Communications House
210 Old Street
London EC1V 9UN

Tel. 0171–490 1447

The above offer a national service, and also have offices in the North
of England and Scotland.

COMPLAINTS ABOUT THE MEDIA

The Press Complaints Commission

1 Salisbury Square
London EC4Y 8AE

Tel. 0171–353 1248

The Broadcasting Complaints Commission

35 and 37 Grosvenor Gardens
London SW1W 0BS

Tel. 0171–630 1966

Campaign for Press and Broadcasting Freedom

96 Dalston Lane
London E8 1NG

Tel. 0171–923 3671

This pressure group, which campaigns for a more accountable and accessible media, can offer advice on right to reply.

FURTHER READING

If your appetite for marketing has been whetted, you may be eager to lay your hands on some further marketing books. There are plenty to choose from: a visit to your nearest reference library or decent academic bookseller will reveal shelves heaving with texts on every aspect of the discipline. There's just one problem; most marketing books are written for commercial bodies. However, there are a few decent texts written specially for the voluntary sector:

VOLUNTARY SECTOR MARKETING

Meeting Need – Successful Charity Marketing by Ian Bruce

Ian Bruce is Director General of RNIB and Director of VOLPROF at City University Business School. Drawing on his 25 years' experience in the voluntary sector, Ian Bruce's book covers the marketing of goods, service provision, campaigning, pressure group activity and fundraising.

Published in 1994 by ICSA/Prentice Hall

Public and Non-Profit Marketing by Christopher Lovelock and Charles Weinberg

This American book covers statutory and voluntary organisation marketing and includes 20 case studies and readings.

2nd edition published in 1989 by the Scientific Press, California

Strategic Marketing for Non-Profit Organisations by Philip Kotler and Alan Andreasen

Kotler, a leading academic in the field of marketing generally, was among the first to see the potential of marketing for the public and voluntary sector – way back in the 1960s.

4th edition published in 1991 by Prentice Hall, New Jersey

GENERAL MARKETING

Marketing Today by Gordon Oliver

This book is more readable than many general marketing texts, though it is still on the heavy side. Unlike many marketing tomes, this does contain a few – though only a few! – pages on voluntary sector marketing (out of over 500 in total).

3rd edition published by Prentice Hall, 1990

INDEX